The Politics of the Internet

The Politics of the Internet

Political Claims-making in Cyberspace and Its Effect on Modern Political Activism

R.J. Maratea

LEXINGTON BOOKS
Lanham • Boulder • New York • Toronto • Plymouth, UK

Published by Lexington Books
A wholly owned subsidiary of Rowman & Littlefield
4501 Forbes Boulevard, Suite 200, Lanham, Maryland 20706
www.rowman.com

10 Thornbury Road, Plymouth PL6 7PP, United Kingdom

British Library Cataloguing in Publication Information Available

Library of Congress Cataloging-in-Publication Data

Maratea, R. J., 1973-
The politics of the Internet : political claimsmaking in cyberspace and its effect on modern political
activism / R.J. Maratea.
pages cm
Includes bibliographical references and index.
ISBN 978-0-7391-7894-2 (cloth : alk. paper) -- ISBN 978-0-7391-7895-9 (electronic)
1. Internet--Political aspects. 2. Internet and activism. 3. Political participation--Technological innovations. I. Title.
HM851.M367 2014
302.23'1--dc23
2013042387

∞™ The paper used in this publication meets the minimum requirements of American
National Standard for Information Sciences Permanence of Paper for Printed Library
Materials, ANSI/NISO Z39.48-1992.

Printed in the United States of America

For Mom Torre, the Ultimate Fanilow

Contents

Acknowledgments

Over the years I have been fortunate to be mentored by some amazing scholars; my thanks can never be adequate repayment for their selfless efforts in helping me achieve my goals. I am not sure why David Altheide and Joel Best invested so much time and energy in my development, but my accomplishments will always be a reflection of their faith in my abilities. I also thank Aaron Kupchik, Aaron Fichtelberg, John Hepburn, Ben Fleury-Steiner, and Lindsay Hoffman for their support. Each of you has imparted upon me a unique and valued perspective, and I have greatly benefited from your expertise and guidance. Tammy Anderson deserves special merit for taking me under her wing and showing me the importance of hard work, exceptional scholarship, and persevering when all you want to do is quit. I am indebted to Brian Monahan, Victor Perez, John Barnshaw, David Keys, and Tom Winfree for taking the time to provide editorial advice even though they were under no obligation to do so; your contributions helped make this project seem a little less overwhelming.

I am also grateful for my colleagues and students at New Mexico State University. The department of Criminal Justice offered me my first teaching position out of graduate school, and I have subsequently been fortunate to meet some extraordinary students who routinely reinvigorate my desire to teach and learn. My colleagues at NMSU, including Carlos Posadas, Robert Duran, David Keys, Dana Greene, Dulcinea Lara, Cynthia Bejarano, Jody Crowley, and Francisco Alatorre, have each offered me guidance as a novice scholar and deserve thanks for putting up with my perpetual grumpiness for the last five years. Additionally, my research assistants, Marco Ortigoza and Joshua Tafoya, provided invaluable help during the data collection stage of this project.

I am fortunate to have a number of friends who are willing to offer advice, encouragement, and support: Brian Owin, Debra D'Agostino, Elizabeth Mansley, Jason Ordini, Ross Kleinstuber, Manuel Torres, Kimber Williams, and the debonair Terry Lilly. Giancarlo Panagia merits thanks for sharing his infectious spirit, positivity, and enthusiasm for life despite being the most underappreciated scholar in academia. There were many times during the writing of this book that Giancarlo got my ideas back on track after my mind had gotten derailed. Likewise, Rebecca Tiger has imparted me with great wisdom on all things related to mass communication and celebrity gossip. I have shamelessly taken many of her ideas and incorporated them into this book. I also wish to express gratitude to Jamie Longazel and Phil Kavanaugh for their many hours watching, discussing, and otherwise obsessing with me over Big Blue during the last ten years; and to John Sullivan, my oldest and closest friend, whose friendship I relentlessly mock, but really do appreciate (and who remembers that I caught his only would-be home run).

The staff at Lexington Books has been tremendously supportive and deserves commendation for their professionalism. Sociology editor Jana Hodges-Kluck has guided me every step of the way through this process; her patience and encouragement has been invaluable, as I have attempted to figure out exactly how to write a book. Jana somehow saw value in the proposal submitted by an unknown assistant professor and gave me the opportunity to complete this project. Whatever happens from here, I owe her more than I can express with a simple thank you. I also would like to acknowledge Sarah Stanton, the sociology editor at Rowman & Littlefield who rejected my proposal but forwarded it Lexington for review. In many ways, everything you are about to read is Sarah's fault.

Finally, I could not have completed this book without the encouragement of my family. They have always supported my endeavors, taught me the importance of optimism (even though I am an unwavering pessimist), and inspired me to move far from home to pursue my goals. Here's to you, Ken Howard!

Preface

This book extends from my experience with Internet technology and my time spent researching all of the ways that mass communication affects our perceptions of social reality. Its origins really date back fourteen years to when I was an eager graduate student fortunate to experience David Altheide's *Crime and Mass Media* seminar at Arizona State University. During that semester I wrote a paper about media coverage of the Columbine school shooting, in which I noted how Mark Manes, who sold guns to Klebold and Harris that were used in the massacre, was described by the press as having gone target shooting with the killers in the weeks prior to the slaughter. At the time I did not think that I had written anything particularly profound, but I can vividly recall David's excited reaction to my work: "You've figured it out! Mass media can alter the direction of time!" You see, news reports had framed Mark Manes as cavorting with ruthless murderers even though his target practice with Klebold and Harris happened before they committed their fateful crimes. In that moment I learned how such simple and subtle framing in news media has a profound implication on the ways we interpret the people, places, and things that make up our social lives.

I am not really sure why that experience resonated so strongly with me, yet it changed the course of my life because I decided to spend my career studying the sociological implications of mass communication, and it ultimately led to the completion of this book. I am not arrogant enough to presume that the information provided on the pages that follow will have as profound an effect on your life as Altheide's words and teaching had on mine. I do hope that you will enjoy the read and learn something interesting along the way.

I

Theoretical Background

Chapter One

The Internet as a Vehicle for Social Change

Communications theorist Marshall McLuhan famously wrote that the medium has become the message. Broadcasting innovations like television, he suggests, have become as important as news and entertainment content itself in understanding the social implications of mass media because they influence how that content is received by the public (McLuhan 1964). At the time of his writing in the 1960s, McLuhan is said to have envisioned the emergence of a World Wide Web by which information could flow rapidly across a proverbial "global" village (Levinson 1999). Of course, McLuhan could never have actually predicted the ubiquity and power of the Internet as a mass medium. Online technology not only allows for real-time interpersonal communication and data retrieval without the limitations of time and space associated with offline social interaction, but also exists as a deregulated public space where no single entity fully regulates the flow of information. Few would argue that the Internet is now an indispensable part of how we communicate, shop, learn, and, more pragmatically, live our lives on a daily—even hourly—basis.

So why is this important? As we have adapted to and become engaged in a wide variety of online environments, the Internet has become host to new sources for news and information that are global in scope. Integral aspects of everyday life now regularly occur in cyberspace: We communicate with people, get news, buy things, pay bills, and can even learn about popular culture or peruse for gossip. All of these experiences have become powerful influences that shape how we perceive the world around us. Some people, whom we may refer to as cyber-optimists (Norris 2001), believe that the Internet has made average citizens more active participants in the acquisition and interpretation of knowledge, and cultivated a democratized public sphere because anyone with an online connection can have a meaningful voice in civic discourse. This very sentiment has been expressed by one of the most recognizable cyber-optimists, former Vice President Al Gore, who has stated that the Internet "holds the great promise of empowering enough individuals who share that broad public interest in an issue like global warming to organize and express themselves with sufficient intensity and focus to overcome the special interests" (Vargas 2009).

Gore's sentiment is by no means unique. Joe Trippi (2004), who managed Howard Dean's 2004 presidential campaign, wrote in his book, *The Revolution Will Not Be Televised*, that the Internet is "the last place where democracy [stands] a chance" (viii). Perhaps it is not surprising, then, that numerous journalists in recent years have pointed to the mass uprisings in places like Brazil, Tunisia, Egypt, Moldova, and Iran as evidence that online technology helps hasten the democratization process. It was matter-of-factly stated in *The New Yorker* magazine that "Facebook and Twitter have undoubtedly accelerated the protests by spreading news that would otherwise have taken a long time to spread, by quickly connecting people who aren't generally able to connect in authoritarian countries and by inflaming passions" (Thompson 2011). CNN even went so far as to suggest calling the 2010 citizen revolt in Tunisia "a Facebook revolution" (Taylor 2011).

Most likely you have heard similar statements about the Internet transforming some other aspect of social life—perhaps one more directly related to your own life. In fact, a simple keyword search on Google yields millions of results about the potential for online technology to revolutionize everything from shopping to television, automobiles, Islam, and far more other things than there is space to mention. Thanks to the Internet, so the argument goes, audiences now have at their disposal a seemingly infinite number of online news sources, many of which are published independent of the mass press and facilitate greater access to knowledge and information. Some claim that this trend reflects a collapse in the *gatekeeping* authority of Big Media (Williams and Delli Carpini 2000, 2004); that is, the monopoly that news workers have in establishing social and cultural agendas, determining what issues are newsworthy, and influencing public opinion. In the New Media world, anyone with a computer and an Internet connection has the potential to publish his or her views to audiences that were once the exclusive province of mainstream news agencies like CNN and *The New York Times*.

From a sociological perspective, the implications of such a dynamic shift in media culture are profound. Because information flows more freely in cyberspace without the constraints of mass media oversight or government censorship (in democratized states, at least, where political leaders have been hesitant to repress the Internet), we are left to wonder the extent to which news organizations will maintain their clout as cultural gatekeepers. It is well understood among scholars that journalists are a powerful force in shaping popular perceptions about social issues.[1] In particular, we are aware that media play an important role in determining how and why things come to be recognized as socially relevant in the public consciousness. After all, phenomena like global warming and racism do not simply exist in a vacuum waiting for us to discover them. Instead, activists make claims about those conditions in hopes of redirecting our attention toward the perceived threat. This process of *claims-making* is intended to spark civic outrage, rally supporters into action, and ultimately force the powers that be into taking the proper action to rectify the problem (Spector and Kitsuse 1977).[2]

Historically, the most effective way for claims-makers to accomplish this task is by piggybacking protest efforts on a crystallizing event (e.g., rising autism diagnoses in children as a platform to vilify the use of vaccines, advocating for passage of the Patriot Act after 9/11, and so forth), or by engaging in street-level demonstrations like sit-ins, and marches. Draft card burnings during the Vietnam War, the 1963 march on Washington, D.C., for civil rights, and even the recent Tea Party rallies are all examples of high-profile events designed to pique public interest. The constant need for novel material means the press is generally receptive to these types of attention-grabbing tactics; yet it also allows news workers to function as a filtering mechanism: Coverage raises awareness to newsworthy issues, while unsuccessful activism is frequently ignored by journalists. Claims-making, therefore, is predicated by need for media exposure that publicizes concerns to the larger population of distressed citizens.

The Internet seemingly changes this paradigm because it is fundamentally different from all preceding mass communication technologies. The reasons—and the results, both realized and potential—as they pertain to our collective understandings of political issues and activism are the focus of this book. In a nutshell, the Internet can be accessed around the clock from remote locations, allowing users to obtain news and information anywhere they can acquire an access signal. Plus, vast amounts of data can be transmitted globally at incomprehensible speeds from a theoretically infinite amount of available online space. Of course, the Internet yields a flood of information, much of which will never be sifted through by any given person; thus filtering mechanisms like search engines have become essential when navigating the morass of web pages, blogs, and Yahoos found in cyberspace. Yet amidst this plethora of content, all sorts of regular people who have historically been excluded from mass media are now empowered to become "citizen journalists" with a global platform to engage in political activism. We no longer are limited to watching the television news or reading the daily paper to learn about popular perspectives on social and political issues. In the Internet age, we can be that source of news or, at least, access an array of mainstream and independent media sites with the simple click of a mouse.

CYBER-ARENAS AS CLAIMS-MAKING FORUMS

This book will examine how the Internet has emerged as an important vehicle for political claims-making by exploring how activists use online technology to publicize claims to ever-increasing audiences whose potential is enormous, yet not always realized. If you have ever watched television, read a newspaper, or listened to talk radio, then you already understand this process. Consider the tragic oil spill in the Gulf of Mexico that devastated wetlands across the coast of Louisiana and the Gulf Coast during the spring and summer of 2010. In the immediate aftermath, a spokesperson for British Petroleum (in this case, then CEO Tony Heyward), the company whose rig exploded thereby producing the spill, held a press conference at which he mitigated both the effects of the disaster and his own company's liability, as well as offering solutions for "capping" the leaking well. In these highly publicized moments, Heyward was generating claims with the intent of persuading audiences that his company had limited culpability in the disaster. His goal was to redirect or deflect blame for the spill, while concurrently identifying the preferred resolution that should be adopted so that British Petroleum (a victim, per Heyward) could help to solve the problem.

My central argument is that all types of political claims-makers, ranging from corporate leaders like Tony Heyward to citizen journalists, can rapidly publicize a large volume of claims to audiences without first having to receive attention from mainstream journalists. Whereas in the past one would have needed to watch a television newscast or read the morning paper to learn about Heyward's framing of the Gulf oil spill, his words now were instantly scattered across the Internet and made available to us at all times and from almost anywhere. So ubiquitous is cyberspace that it may almost seem like there are an infinite number of access points to get information online about all things political. This is because the Internet functions as a vast collection of interconnected *cyber-arenas* where claims are continuously disseminated to audiences and social reality is in a perpetual state of negotiation. Unlike more traditional modes of news distribution that are fundamentally rigid in nature—print publications have finite column space; television and radio broadcasts have limited airtime—cyber-arenas exist in virtual space and are therefore malleable; they can fluctuate as needed to accommodate additional news space. Part of the dynamism of cyber-arenas is that they are always accessible and in a constant state of information flux; that is, they can be updated with fresh material in real time at any point during the day. By comparison, newspapers, magazines, and other print publications only provide new articles when the latest issues are released. Although television news is available twenty-four hours a day, audiences are only exposed to the information presented on-air at any particular moment. Cyber-arenas simply offer a greater breadth of available information along with affording audiences more options for locating content at their choosing.

THE KEY EFFECTS OF CYBER-ARENAS

Chances are most every Internet user is making use of cyber-arenas in some capacity or another, whether for purposes of political activism or simply to communicate with friends and family using social media. Even for those of us with no inclination to participate in civic matters, the scope of online networking can seem overwhelming when a long lost acquaintance sends you a friend request on Facebook or someone from across the globe responds to a Tweet. Now imagine what that sort of communication power can mean to a political activist who has never before had any sort of social voice, a politician with grand career aspirations, or a news agency seeking to break the next big scandal. Simply having an online presence does not necessarily translate to political or journalistic success; however, it does reflect a measure of idyllic hope that the little guy can use this democratizing force to make the world a better place. To this end, the first key effect is that cyber-arenas are reasonably egalitarian claims-making and protest venues. Because the flow of information online is not yet restricted by corporate, governmental, or institutional editorial structures, nor hindered by the stringent deadline and budgetary restraints associated with mainstream news production, no single entity controls the availability of materials. Furthermore, public officials in Westernized nations have mostly been hesitant to regulate content, leaving the responsibility for monitoring Internet use in the hands of individual users through software that allows for the censoring of unwanted subject matter. This laissez-faire approach is rooted in the principle of Net neutrality, which suggests that all information transmitted over the Internet should be treated equally regardless of its point of origin (Wu 2003). Practically speaking, this means that you should be able to access your favorite blog just as easily as corporate news websites operated by CNN and Fox News.

Second, large volumes of information can be retrieved, passed on, and archived with greater speed and flexibility than is possible using any other form of communication technology. Activists normally rely on time-consuming protest tactics, such as staging high-profile public events or coordinating more subdued letter writing campaigns, to mobilize supporters and draw public attention to their issues. While sometimes effective, these strategies require sufficient resources (e.g., money and manpower), intensive planning, and determined public relations work. Web spaces, by contrast, require minimal effort. Claims can easily be posted online and then efficiently updated around the clock. Perhaps lacking the cachet of grassroots, street-level protest, the Internet has nonetheless allowed some activists to get so far ahead of the media curve that journalists and politicians have been forced to respond. News workers themselves are now so rushed to out-scoop competitors that they have little time to examine their reports for factual accuracy. We saw this firsthand in June of 2013 when both CNN and Fox News reported live on the air and their websites that the Supreme Court had overturned the Affordable Care Act, more commonly known as Obamacare. In their rush to beat the competition, both ended up relaying information to audiences before it could be properly verified as accurate. As it turned out, the Supreme Court had upheld the constitutionality of the law.

Inaccurate reporting that results from the pressure to "break" news is not necessarily a new phenomenon. For instance, the *Chicago Tribune* infamously declared that New York Governor Thomas Dewey had defeated incumbent Harry Truman in the 1948 presidential election, when in actuality he had lost the vote by a considerable margin.[3] The larger issue, however, is that the *immediacy* of information distribution and speed of transmission from point of origin to audience have become the defining ethos of modern media culture. This is precisely why the actual reporting curve has become increasingly compressed even as the news cycle has expanded to 24-hours. Fast-paced websites designed for high-speed Internet connections are well oriented to this environment and can titillate audiences with an abundance of fresh, newsworthy, and breaking stories. They also allow these reports to remain available online long after their original publication or broadcast date. Thus, it is not just the variety of content or the speed with which people can access information in cyberspace that differentiates the Internet from other forms of communication media, it is also the ability to archive material that is no longer available via print, television, and radio. Stories that have to be edited out to fit the standard "news hole" may therefore be retained in cyberspace and stored for future availability.

Third, the Internet provides activists with greater flexibility when distributing claims and coordinating protest action, which may help raise public awareness and attract media attention. Because the Internet functions simultaneously as an information sharing and networking structure, activists who were previously excluded from (or had limited access to) mass media now have a powerful and relatively inexpensive communication platform to advance their issues. Of course, the "carrying capacity" of the Internet is not really infinite; limitations exist in terms of the costs associated with maintaining a web space and the amount of time that activists can dedicate to updating their sites with fresh content. Additionally, most claims will likely remain niche concerns without ever attaining widespread recognition because publishing information in cyberspace does not necessarily mean that news workers and the larger population more generally, will pay any attention (Hilgartner and Bosk 1988). Hence, it is unclear whether the average person will recognize relevant protest and claims-making action that is oc-

curring in cyberspace without being prompted to do so by a dedicated supporter, the press, or some other external force.

Fourth, the Internet gives audiences greater control to search for news and
information at their choosing and according to their specific areas of interest.
Most of us can be described as passive news consumers. We do not necessarily create news; rather, we tend to retrieve reports manufactured by trusted
Big Media sources (Hargittai 2004). Online technology, however, makes us
less bound to mainstream news because the Internet is replete with millions
of readily accessible alternative and independent sites that provide information not covered by the press (Fallows and Rainie 2004). For example, the
Internet has made it possible to view graphic photos and videos deemed
inappropriate by network news standards, such as the execution footage of
former Iraqi dictator Saddam Hussein. While this does not mean that we have
unfettered access to everything online, it suggests that we can more actively
locate all sorts of materials that we may never have been exposed to in earlier
times. Of course, more recently when former Libyan dictator Muammar
Gaddafi was executed and then defiled by a mob of civilian rebels, Big
Media outlets aired the footage of his corpse virtually unedited on broadcast
television newscasts and their websites. This is, perhaps, a direct response to
"audience grabbing" from autonomous online sites that are neither bound by
Federal Communications Commission (FCC) oversight nor required to censor indecent imagery. It may also indicate that the press has had to adjust
how news is presented to accommodate the fact that individuals can use the
Internet to learn all they need to know without ever perusing a traditional
news source.

Fifth, there are fundamental issues of trust, deception, and safety inherent
to online communication. If you have ever received an e-mail from a Niger-
ian prince about the monetary fortunes that await you if you send a small
down payment to release the withheld funds, then you are already aware of
how easy it is to assume a false persona or spread lies under the guise of
objective truth in cyberspace without ever having to reveal your true self.
While this may not be problematic for individuals who covet anonymity,
activists neither presume nor desire that what they publish will remain private despite the fact that their actual identities may be unknown to prospective readers. Just the opposite: activists "would like theirs to be the message
that is attended to, recalled, or acted upon" (Wathen and Burkell 2002, 134).
Claims-makers must therefore develop strategies for establishing trust in
order to build a loyal following and confirm their standing as reliable
sources. Credibility in cyberspace, after all, is not necessarily "a characteristic of a source, medium, or message, but is dependent on the perceptions of
the receiver" (Johnson et al. 2007, 101).[4] In other words, political activists in
online environments are no less reliant on producing messages that resonate
as culturally relevant with the general public than when protesters were

marching for civil rights or burning draft cards in opposition to the Vietnam War.

Finally, there are stability concerns in cyberspace. With the Internet still in its relative infancy as a mass medium, we must consider the sustainability of online forums, the long-term viability of web-based protest tactics, and, in a more general sense, how activists can best position themselves for success in cyberspace. Blogs, for example, have seen a precipitous rise in popularity in recent years; but there are no guarantees that blogs will continue to exist in their current form or remain culturally relevant. This is not to suggest that online communication will diminish. Rather, what is popular today may be obsolete tomorrow; as rapidly as a MySpace becomes socially relevant, a Facebook just as quickly replaces it. Verne Kopytoff (2011) notes in *The New York Times* that there is already evidence that blog creation and usage is starting to decline as more people shift their interest to social media sites like Twitter. Given the volatility of a swiftly changing cyberspace, political activists may have to continually reassess the tactics they currently employ in cyberspace, as well as develop new techniques for conducting business online if they intend to remain viable in the future.

Throughout the book we will address these issues in order to identify whether the Internet is really all that revolutionary, and whether historically influential claims-making groups, such as corporate lobbyists, are actually best positioned to succeed in a supposedly democratized new media world. Digital technology may provide a dynamic, low-cost vehicle for political claims-making on a global scale that is accessible to a greater number of people than has ever been possible using the printing press, radio, or television, but it cannot guarantee that anyone will actually pay attention to those claims. To address this point, we will also examine whether the dynamics of social power in the public sphere have fundamentally changed from previous eras. Practically speaking, do the powerful continue to influence public opinion while the powerless, for the most part, remain disenfranchised? If so, it would indicate that agenda setting for practitioners in a wide range of fields, from medicine to social welfare to criminal justice, has yet to be *greatly* impacted by Internet technology and citizen journalism. Thus, an important point for consideration as you proceed through this book is whether cyber-arenas are indeed producing a democratic global village wherein political activists with varying degrees of social power all have a meaningful voice in the mass-mediated, public sphere.

PLAN FOR THE BOOK

Structurally, this book is divided into three sections. The first outlines the theoretical framework, including a conceptualization of cyber-arenas that addresses how political claims-makers, news personnel, and communication technology each play an important role in constructing how we make sense of social life. Chapter 2 situates the book in the literature on symbolic interactionism, which suggests that social life is constructed primarily through language. As we communicate with each other and receive mediated messages from claims-makers, politicians, and news workers, to name a few, we are actively being socialized to see the world around us in ways that allow our reality—or, at least, how we perceive reality—to take shape. Specifically, the chapter examines how news coverage and communication technology influence the meanings that we attach to political issues by focusing on how claimants use those media to strategically disseminate information using rhetoric that is designed to manipulate our individual and collective perceptions. What we will see is that our ideas and opinions about politics are rarely if ever purely our own; they are instead in a constant state of persuasion by political actors trying to convince us to support their agendas.

The second section shifts to *emergent* forms of political claims-making and activism that are unique to cyberspace. Specifically, we will assess the idea that the Internet has been a "game changer" for average people by examining both the influence of amateur claimants in online settings and the development of new forms of cyber-protest. Chapter 3 focuses on the rise of "citizen journalism" and its affect on mass media and political culture, as well as an analysis of the degree to which layperson news work is truly influencing modern politics. Specific attention is paid to the 2004 "Rathergate" scandal, which legitimized political bloggers as credible news sources and exemplifies how successful citizen journalism can augment conventional reporting practices. Subsequently, we have been witness to the birth of social networking, wherein anyone with an Internet connection and a Facebook or Twitter account has a virtual soapbox to distribute claims and voice opinions about a whole host of political matters. While the impact of these developments is profound and has fundamentally altered civic participation in mass media, most citizen journalists nonetheless languish in cyber-obscurity. This chapter will therefore explore the specific factors that contribute to effective citizen journalism, while noting why citizen-generated claims typically fail to maintain (or even attain) long-term public interest.

Chapter 4 examines the burgeoning field of political cyber-protest, or activism that is organized and performed primarily, if not exclusively, in cyberspace. These "dot causes" (Clark and Themudo 2006) have attained a great deal of attention in recent years because they operate fundamentally differently than a traditional "brick-and-mortar" social movements. In particular, attention will be focused on the release of classified government documents via the web space WikiLeaks, which has come to represent the egalitarian potential of Internet technology by exposing how governments have been unable (or unwilling) to control the flow of information in cyberspace.

This chapter will show that for all its notoriety, WikiLeaks has only achieved marginal success. While the site has been credited with cultivating dissent and even full-fledged revolutions abroad, its influence in most Westernized nations has been minimized due an online organizational structure that fails to cultivate a widespread, endearing cultural response, combined with scattered, inconsistent, and unflattering media coverage.

The third section of the book focuses on the ways that *institutionalized* political claims-making groups, such as social movement organizations and lobbyists, use the Internet to communicate with supporters, mobilize both support and financial resources, and build clout among policymakers. Chapter 5 explores how social movement organizations employ cyber-arenas as a networking structure to distribute claims and interact directly with followers. The chapter focuses specifically on the Tea Party movement, which has garnered considerable public attention in recent years by advancing the idea that excessive federal government is infringing on citizens' rights in the United States. The Tea Party movement provides a useful point of analysis because it allows us to trace the growth of a modern political movement and better understand why the formation of advocacy networks in cyberspace is consequential for political activists. In this case, we will see that the Internet facilitates communication, provides a new channel for building important coalitions, and supports virtual spaces where supporters can congregate and insulate themselves from critics that may challenge their credibility. These benefits notwithstanding, the chapter will ultimately show that the Tea Party's success is owed in large part to its corporate "backing" and origins in street-level protest, which attracted media and political interest that legitimized the movement.

Even with an online networking structure in place, political claims-making campaigns are doomed to fail if activists are unable to acquire needed resources and mobilize supporters into action. Historically, protest tactics have centered on attention-grabbing public events like marches or sit-ins that redirect public interest to a group's cause. Chapter 6 focuses on how institutionalized political claims-making groups, such as lobbying firms, have developed online protest tactics that tend to be much more passive in nature than traditional forms of grassroots activism. Using the National Rifle Association (NRA) as a case study, we will see how mobilization efforts begin with dramatic anecdotes that describe how supporter contributions lead to tangible results in the fight against "Second Amendment enemies" and corrupt politicians who seek to "take away your guns." Audiences are then directed to participate in a form of protest characterized by individual action accomplished from the comfort of home or any other private setting. By examining the NRA, we can identify four core elements of cyber-mobilization: (1) online demonstrations; (2) fundraising to subsidize lobbying and media functions; (3) contacting public officials and corporate leaders; and (4) organizing protest efforts at the community level. Taken collectively, these components are helping to reshape our understanding of how claims-makers mobilize support because they diverge from the types of attention-grabbing protest tactics that activists have historically used to obtain media interest. Consequently, more established "insiders" with stable resources and powerful political connections, such as corporate lobbyists and groups like the NRA, might ultimately be best positioned to benefit from Internet technology.

Chapter 7 will discuss the important role played by the press in the political process. News workers selectively filter which stories are presented to audiences and determine how those issues, events, and actors are framed, oftentimes through narrative tales that are geared more toward entertainment value than intellectual analysis. Not surprisingly, then, news agencies have developed innovative new techniques for presenting information that are oriented toward the immediacy and the drama of breaking news. We will also see that the public is no less reliant on the mainstream media to learn about political affairs than they were prior to the advent of the Internet. Despite all of the new and independent sources that have cropped up online, the press may actually be using the Internet to expand its role as gatekeepers; audiences who use alternative web sources may often do so *after* professional journalists have exposed them to a given issue.

The final chapter will begin with a review of the central questions, issues, and concepts discussed in the book, along with summarizing the "Internet effect" on political activism specifically and the culture of modern politics more generally. This discussion will be supplemented by placing the Internet in historical context with other forms of communication technology in order to establish a point of comparison with previous innovations that were similarly hailed as democratizing forces. The conclusion will also explore the continued relevance of online technology and cyber-arenas on the future of both grassroots and institutionalized political activism, and long-term implications for successful protest, by providing some current examples that exemplify the intersections that exist online between activism and social power. Specific attention will be paid to the ways that changes to the availability and consumption of information affect popular understandings of cultural issues and the distribution of cultural authority in an increasingly interconnected digital world.

NOTES

1. The literature describing how social reality is shaped by news workers is quite extensive. Some of the more notable work in this area includes: Altheide 1995, 2002; Altheide and Snow 1979; Couch 1984; Fishman 1980; Glassner 1999; Iyengar and Kinder 1987; MacKuen and Coombs 1981; McLuhan 1960; Monahan 2010; and Snow 1983.

2. Spector and Kitsuse (1977) base their understanding of claims-making in the constructionist perspective that social problems do not exist objectively, but rather are "the activities of individuals or groups making assertions of grievances and claims with respect to some putative conditions" (75). Claims-making activities generate those assertions, regardless of whether the resulting claims are valid or erroneous (76). Social problems, therefore, emerge as a by-product of claims-making and only exist to the extent that people define particular conditions or phenomena as problematic.

3. Truman would famously celebrate his victory by being photographed holding a copy of the *Tribune* that erroneously proclaimed his defeat.

4. See also Berlo, Lemert and Mertz 1969.

Chapter Two

Constructing Reality in Cyberspace

During the second Red Scare that began in the late 1940s, Senator Joseph McCarthy prompted considerable public fear by warning that the rise of communism around the world was being accompanied by traitorous disloyalty of "enemies from within," whom he characterized as American citizens with extreme leftist associations and liberal political leanings. The resulting period of heightened anti-communism became defined by the widespread practice of McCarthyism, which involved making accusations of disloyalty and even treason without just cause. We know in retrospect that McCarthy's concerns were exaggerated and mostly inspired by the electoral gain that he and his supporters received by preying on public fears and publicizing unsubstantiated claims of traitorous behavior against his political opponents. His targets, however, suffered greatly; many were "blackballed" and unable to gain meaningful employment, while others were unjustly imprisoned. Given this historical context, perhaps we should not be surprised when present-day politicians like Michelle Bachmann publically suggest that we should "take a great look at the views of the people in Congress and find out are they pro-America or anti-America" (MSNBC 2008), or when Indiana Senate candidate Richard Mourdock claimed during the 2012 election that pregnancy from rape is "something that God intended to happen" (Madison 2012). Public officials have long been prone to make ideological statements—however egregious and irrational they may seem—that pander to their voting base by preaching to exaggerated fears about all the social harms that will come to pass if we stray from the moral and religious path, or if the politicians on the other side of the aisle have their way.

The real problem is not that the bulk of Americans explicitly buy into these types of claims. The dismal approval ratings of Congress tend to suggest a prevailing disgust about how the game of politics is presently being played. Yet, elected officials are rarely voted out of office, and in recent years politicians seem apt to make public statements that are polarizing, lacking in intellectual merit, and often diverging from reality. Equally disconcerting is the fact that mainstream political news coverage seems to be following the same tract, thereby fragmenting audiences along ideological lines toward media outlets that offer partisan filtering rather than objective and informative analysis (Baum and Groeling 2008). To the extent that political beliefs influence where people get their news, it stands to reason that there is a growing audience being selectively exposed to a disproportionate number of claims that merely reinforce what they want to believe is true irrespective of fact or empirical evidence (Prior 2005; Stroud 2010).[1]

POLITICAL CLAIMS IN A POST-FACT SOCIETY

You may recall the moment during the 2008 presidential election campaign when a woman at a John McCain rally told the Arizona senator that she "can't trust Obama" because "he's an Arab." A few minutes earlier during that same assembly, McCain was actually booed by his own supporters for telling a man in the audience that Barack Obama was a decent man and "someone that you do not have to be scared of as President of the United States." These examples are not intended to ridicule Republicans, but rather illustrate that a political and media culture constructed on hyperbole, incivility, and fear influences how a good percentage of the public perceive civic life. The fact that McCain's attempt at interjecting reason was met with scorn by his own backers speaks to the fact that "when fear is the prevailing framework for looking at social issues, then other competing frames and discourses lose out" (Altheide and Michalowski 1999, 476). Among the more tangible consequences is the widespread distrust among audiences of both politicians and fellow citizens that hold differing perspectives, and the prevalence by which those groups are characterized as less intelligent, un-American, or any other moniker that identifies them as somehow being dangerous to our collective welfare. Thus, Arizona Senator John Kyl's erroneous claim that "well over 90 percent" of Planned Parenthood's business came from abortions effectively provided rhetorical ammunition to supporters in the fight to overturn *Roe v. Wade*, even though he later redacted the statement by claiming it was not intended to be factual (Peralta 2011). Likewise, when Representative Alan Grayson told Congress that Republicans' idea of health care reform is to make sick people "die quickly," he was trying to manipulate the debate by making an emotional contrast without any basis in fact between heartless conservative politicians and compassionate Democrats who intend to make sure everyone has access to medical care.

We may reasonably assume that politicians like Kyl and Grayson know that they are lying or deliberately spreading false truths when they utter embellished statements about social issues and political opponents. Yet they also realize that media outlets will respond to hyperbole by reporting their words. In the past, this might have meant having a sound bite played on the evening news. Today, however, politically motivated overstatements are splashed across cable news and Internet headlines, while partisan filtering seems to increasingly frame the ideologically charged discourse and debates orchestrated by recognizable personalities like Bill O'Reilly and Rachel Maddow. For claims-makers, this heightened news platform helps gets their message out to sympathetic audiences that are apt to agree regardless of whether the declarations they espouse are factually accurate. Farhad Manjoo (2008) attributes this to the reality of living in a post-fact digital world where the enormity of information availability gives individuals greater authority to seek out what they believe by finding news sources with the messages that suit them, "whether sophisticated or naïve, extremist or banal, grounded in reality or so far out you're floating in an asteroid belt, among people who feel the exact same way" (2). Among the biggest effects of such information diversity is that truth no longer exists objectively, but is instead constructed from the "facts" that we choose to accept or ignore.

> No longer are we holding opinions different from one another; we're also holding different facts . . . the creeping partisanship has begun to distort our very perceptions about what is "real" and what isn't. Indeed, you can go so far as to say we're now fighting over competing versions of reality. And it is more convenient than ever before for some of us to live in a world built out of our own facts (Manjoo 2008, 2).

For Manjoo, the seminal issue is the ease by which opinion can now be certified as fact, thereby allowing most anyone to become a lay expert by simply going out and finding information online that validates his or her beliefs, even if it contradicts established scientific truth.

The resulting dismissal of intellectualism is not necessarily a new phenomenon (see Hofstadter 1963); however, we can identify two noteworthy shifts in media culture that have exacerbated the trend away from reasoned analysis and civilized discourse. First, the advent of online and digital technologies makes vast amounts of information perpetually available, much of which lacks any sort of credibility but may nonetheless be accepted as accurate. Second, modern news coverage has become centered on instances and events that offer considerable novelty and shock value (Lundman 2003) while simultaneously affording news workers greater leeway to interject themselves into storylines by taking moral and ideological stands on how we should interpret issues of social and political importance (Altheide 1992). In this sort of a media environment, people can more easily find information that confirms their beliefs, and news personnel are granted greater editorial license to impress their own personal political views upon audiences (Maratea and Monahan 2013).

There was a time when journalists' primary responsibility was to chronicle the day's events with a veneer of objectivity; opinion making was generally limited to a few op-eds and perhaps the efforts of newspaper columnists. This was why it was so shocking when during the 1968 Democratic National Convention, viewers of NBC News heard anchor David Brinkley utter "atta boy, Abe," in response to Connecticut Senator Abraham Ribicoff criticizing Chicago Mayor Richard Daley and the city's police force for using "Gestapo" tactics against Vietnam War protesters (Farber 1988). Brinkley was unaware that his microphone was on when he made clear his feelings. His comment, however, is tame by comparison to the partisanship that has become so endemic in today's news media. Take the explicit praise that Glenn Beck bestowed on controversial Arizona Sheriff Joe Arpaio during a 2007 CNN interview: "I've got to tell you, Sheriff, and I mean this with all due respect: man, I love you. I'd vote for you" (Arpaio and Sherman 2008, 220). In another instance, Fox News contributor Andrea Tantaros cheekily declared during a radio broadcast that listeners should physically assault people that voted for President Obama, whose administration she compared to totalitarian Soviet regimes:

> This is Obama's America. It's like the Soviet Union. He said he would change the country. He said it . . . and a lot of people voted for him. And if you see any of those people today, do me a favor and punch them in the face (Connelly 2013).

Regardless of whether these types of hyperbolic narratives are made seriously or merely said tongue-in-cheek, they exemplify how news workers present political issues as a matter of public spectacle, where they identify the issues or problems—often using seditious rhetoric—and then position themselves as the moral crusaders who tell you what to believe and whose ideas to support (see Altheide 1992).[2]

POLITICAL NEWS WITH A TWIST OF TRUTHINESS

Back in the 1970s, Hunter S. Thompson coined the term "gonzo" to describe a style of journalism that defies conventional reporting standards in favor of beguiling narratives written from the perspective of the authors. Merging both fact and fiction, gonzo journalists do not attempt to detach themselves from their analysis, instead placing themselves as integral characters in their own storylines, often while telling a caustic tale of some shocking event or experience. Based on the "idea that the best fiction is far more true than any kind of journalism" (Thompson 1980, 114), Thompson recognized that the style of gonzo writing he defined and later popularized in his own work is fundamentally different in composition from traditional news work, which requires greater fact-finding, investigation, external verification, and objectivity when reporting facts. Or, at least, that used to be the case. Today when you tune into television news, listen to political talk radio, or read a political blog, chances are what you see and hear will seem a lot like gonzo journalism.

The consequences of this shift in news presentation go beyond simply identifying a declining standard of political analysis in today's media. Americans that watch cable news tend not only to be less informed about current events than people who read *The New York Times* or listen to National Public Radio, but they also exhibit a knowledge deficiency compared to viewers of *The Daily Show*, a satirical news program hosted by comedian Jon Stewart. Even worse, polling indicates that ignoring current events entirely facilitates a greater understanding of civic matters than watching cable news!

> The results show us that there is something about watching Fox News that leads people to do worse on [poll] questions than those who don't watch any news at all . . . The kicker is that MSNBC didn't do all that much better. In one question, some 11 percent of MSNBC viewers actually believed that Occupy Wall Street protesters were Republicans compared to just 3% of Fox viewers . . . ideological media does a very poor job overall . . . they don't challenge people's assumptions. In traditional news, you will find that more often than not, there actually is a correct answer and there is not gray area. People who tune into ideological media are motivated to hear their side of the debate (Rapoza 2011).[3]

Imbalanced coverage effectively insulates people from having to genuinely consider opposing perspectives—even if they are not actively attempting to do so—by exposing them to one-sided framings that are presented in authoritative, but not necessarily factually accurate ways.

All of this brings us to the concept of "truthiness," the word invented by Stephen Colbert in 2005 to describe "truth that comes from the gut" without consideration of facts, logic, and intellectual scrutiny (see Meyer 2009). What this essentially means is that people tend to reach resolute or forceful conclusions in support of—or opposition to—a particular standpoint while failing to factually defend their position. While this may indicate that a person cannot explain the logic behind their argument, it also suggests that when efforts are made to defend the stance in question, individuals merely present a few confirming accounts that are sufficient to validate their beliefs even if they are not empirically or scientifically adequate to verify their claims (Ladyman 2002).[4] Although satirical in its origins, the concept of truthiness has real-world implications to the extent that it helps cultivate what has been described as the "smart idiot" effect: People, regardless of education and literacy, become less persuadable by intellectual arguments and practical evidence in determining what is a "fact" (see Mooney 2012).

The "smart idiot" effect essentially means that when claimants' positions are discredited, "the more committed they will get to those doctrines" (Krugman 2012). Not surprisingly, then, when people are exposed to the flaws in their reasoning, they often "tend to attack the information rather than reconsider their positions" (Niven 2002, 672).[5] Take, for instance, a February 6, 2013, segment from Fox News Channel's *The O'Reilly Factor* that was subsequently published on the network's website, in which host Bill O'Reilly railed against the nation's public school system for being lax on disciplinary standards and cultivating a nationwide "epidemic of disrespect." Today's youth, he argues, show no deference for authority figures like parents, judges, and, presumably, cable news personalities. Ironically, O'Reilly has made a career of calling anyone with whom he disagrees a "pinhead," and in this segment he belittles the efforts of public school employees, as well as a guest who had the audacity to question his supposition that children's behavioral development is influenced more by school officials than parents. Despite presenting no empirical data to back up his claims that disrespectful behavior is endemic in youngsters, O'Reilly nonetheless identifies the problem, its causes (public school officials and political liberals that do not believe in discipline), and the preferred solutions (send your children to Catholic schools).

For O'Reilly and other cable news hosts like Nancy Grace and Ed Schultz, the goal is not objective fact-finding, but rather to perform as a carnival barker of sorts, directing you to step right up and see how the people they dislike and disagree with are destroying the world (Monahan and Maratea 2013). In playing this role, they show us that news workers and their guests can validate the objectivity of their arguments without any verification of fact beyond telling you that their claims are true. Consider this exchange between filmmaker Michael Moore and MSNBC host S.E. Cupp on the prevalence of gun crime from a May 17, 2013, episode of *Real Time with Bill Maher*:

> Bill Maher (host): Let me ask you this: Why has gun homicide gone down in the age of less gun control?
>
> Cupp: As gun ownership has gone up and gun crime has gone down.
>
> Moore: All crime has gone down. That's the answer to this. It's not about the gun crime.
>
> Cupp: It is about the gun crime.

Moore: All crime, ever since Bill Clinton became President crime started going down and it kept going down.

Cupp: But, gun control advocates try to make the link that more guns make for more crime. That is not an intellectually honest argument.

Moore: No . . . since Columbine it makes for another 30 or 40 mass shootings.

Cupp: Mass shootings are also down.

Moore: No!

Cupp: Yes they are!

Maher: Hey, wait. This may be true.

Cupp: It is true.

Maher: We can't go by anecdotal evidence.

Cupp: It is fact. They are down, as is gun crime. That's a fact.

Maher: If that's the fact, we gotta go by the facts.

Cupp: Look it up. I'm not the first person to say it.

Moore: Yes, there's been less school shootings since Columbine. Yes, let me just ponder that for a second.

Cupp: There have been fewer mass shootings over the past 30 years That's just a fact.

This exchange is particularly interesting because you have the host, Bill Maher, acknowledging the need for facts as his guests present competing claims about the prevalence of mass shootings. Yet neither Cupp nor Moore offers any sources to validate their arguments, other than directing the audience to "look it up." At one point, Moore asserts that a dog offers as much protection as a gun during a home invasion, while Cupp explains her expertise on the issue as stemming from the fact that she owns guns: "I have lived and breathed this issue personally for a decade . . . I just happen to be informed on gun issues, unlike most people who talk about them."

Perhaps it is true that gun ownership is tantamount to expertise on the criminological research pertaining to gun crime. Still, there is an inherent superficiality to this debate, with audiences being left to decide whether

Moore or Cupp spewed the most factual facts. As Figure 2.1 shows, an analysis of mass shootings over the last 30 years conducted by *Mother Jones* does not necessarily indicate that mass shootings have been declining since 1982 (Follman, Aronsen, and Pan 2012).[6] How you interpret the numbers, however, determines whether Cupp's argument is indeed correct. In his book *Mass Murder in the United States*, Grant Duwe (2007) identifies only 21 mass shootings between the years 1900–1966, which would seem to indicate that these types of crimes have increased considerably since the middle of the twentieth century. Yet, he also notes that there has been a precipitous decline in public mass shootings from the 1990s (43 cases) to the first decade of the twenty-first century, which only registered 26 such events (Duwe 2007, see also Pearce 2012).[7]

So, was Cupp wrong in her assertion? No, but she was not being factually honest, either. Depending on the timeline you use and how you manipulate the data, you can argue that mass shootings are both increasing and decreasing. At the very least, these sorts of crimes tend to fluctuate higher in some years and then dip lower for no readily apparent reason (see Figure 2.1). In other words, prevalence rates are not necessarily correlated with the level of firearm ownership, gun control legislation, or anything else for that matter. Thus, while it may seem reasonable that S.E. Cupp based her argument against gun control on the declining number of mass shootings, or that Michael Moore pushed for greater regulation by insisting that such incidents are escalating, both positions lacked intellectual depth and failed to grasp the

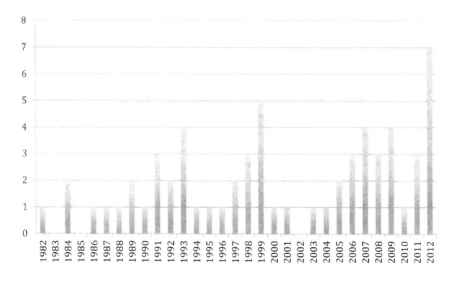

Figure 2.1.   Public Mass Shootings by Year, 1982–2012. Source: *Mother Jones*.

complexities that issues like gun control require in order to make an informed determination.

CLAIMS-MAKING AND THE CONSTRUCTION OF SOCIAL REALITY

The larger point to be made is that understanding issues like the causes of gun crime and their relationship to firearm regulation requires a nuanced assessment that is increasingly difficult to find in traditional and online mass media where public policy is discussed and debated. It is not simply that news coverage fails to accommodate longwinded, scholarly assessments of social and political matters, but also that claims-makers (activists, advocates, pundits, and so forth) are not necessarily interested in using their media platform to relay information that is factually accurate. Although the appearance of credibility is essential for establishing trust, their primary concern is presenting claims that journalists find suitable to report in a standard news story (see Gans 1979). One of the more common ways this is accomplished is by emphasizing that our morality and shared values demand that we give proper attention to a particular political or social problem. Shaping claims in this way not only attracts the sympathy of people who share those beliefs, but also invokes the consternation of critics, whose hostile responses help configure those claims toward news practices that "give preference to stories featuring conflict, outrage, and novelty, making the rhetoric of rectitude ideal for bringing new problems to public attention" (Best 1990, 43–44).

Another way to think about the practice of claims-making is through the lens of *emotions talk*, which reflects discourse "that evaluates and judges; that creates, reinforces, and challenges moral meanings" (Schneider 1984, 182) while simultaneously shaping "preferred emotional orientations" (Loseke 2003, 123). Because impassioned moral pleas draw on familiar language and values that resonate culturally (Berns 2009), claimants can strategically infuse these elements into their rhetoric with the explicit hope of evoking a strong visceral reaction that entices journalists to acknowledge the claims and rallies support among the citizenry.

> A claims-maker can make everyone in the audience feel that he or she has a vested interest in the problem's solution. . . . By characterizing a problem in terms of an individual's experiences, the claims-maker helps the audience imagine how they might respond under the same circumstances. The portrait may invite sympathy and understanding, or it may encourage the audience to feel that they would never succumb to the same pressures or temptations; in either case, the problem becomes less abstract, the claims easier to comprehend (Best 1990, 31, 41).

Oftentimes making claims relatable to audiences requires more than simply appealing to logic; it involves putting forward moral evaluations that are guided by claimants' own personal interests, values, and experiences (Ibarra and Kitsuse 2003; Loseke 2000; Spector and Kitsuse 1977). To the degree that claims-makers can invoke cultural dialogues that alter "in degree or quality an emotion or feeling" (Hochschild 1979, 561), they become better positioned to attract public attention regardless of whether they are attempting to intellectually inform us about the nature, practice, and consequences of a given political issue.

Reality, then, takes shape when journalists elect to disregard certain claims and circulate others that invoke preferred cultural values, beliefs, and norms. For example, take the issue of capital punishment, which the late Justice William Brennan noted in the landmark Supreme Court decision *Furman v. Georgia* (1972), is debated as much, if not more so, on moral and emotional grounds than the pragmatic merits of execution. Similarly, Justice Thurgood Marshall speculated that most citizens would oppose state-sanctioned executions if they truly understood the nature, process, and consequences of capital punishment (Bohm, Vogel, and Maisto 1993, 30). His *Marshall Hypothesis* is predicated on the assumption that most people have a deficit of factual understanding, yet nonetheless reach very forceful and seemingly reasonable conclusions about the merits and necessity of the death penalty (Bohm 2007).[8] At the foundation of Marshall's premise is a fundamental dichotomy: The more informed a populace is about the death penalty, the less likely that society as a whole can maintain support for its constitutionality. Although this contention might be true, reforming public policy and shifting social perceptions is never that cut-and-dry.

In fact, most Americans support capital punishment despite strong empirical evidence that extralegal factors like race and class disproportionately affect disenfranchised and otherwise powerless defendants, increasing the likelihood that prosecutors will seek the death penalty in such cases, that juries will convict and sentence them to death, and that they may one day be exonerated of the crime that led them to being put on death row. While public opinion may ultimately be guided by a lack of knowledge about capital punishment as Marshall suggested, claims-makers and news workers also play a central role in shaping our perceptions of reality about phenomena like the death penalty. Most of us are only confronted with the idea of executions during high-profile murder cases when we are told the harrowing details of crimes so obscene that proponents argue the only mechanism to achieve justice and bring closure to victims' families is to seek the offender's death. At other times we learn of someone being released from death row, or of a Troy Davis being executed despite insufficient evidence to confirm guilt, prompting abolitionists to proclaim the system is broken.

In these highly emotional times—when vile offenders are facing execution or when the wrongly convicted are exonerated—the press tends "to cover the death penalty's popularity without caveats, limitations, or mention of support for alternative sentences" (Niven 2002, 672). Cultural dialogues about capital punishment are thus couched within evocative rhetoric espoused by claimants in the most moralistic of ways, and then transferred to news audiences without accurately contextualizing the underlying moral and ethical dilemmas of such a uniquely severe sanction. In other words, the prevailing media logic (Altheide and Snow 1979) that guides how crime news is reported subsequently fuels public outrage over particular criminal events and often precedes "public outcries for executions" (Vollum and Buffington-Vollum 2010, 18). What emerges from this toxic mix of emotional claims-making and superficial media analysis are popularized narratives that eschew thoughtful analysis and instead reduce complex issues like capital punishment into "morality policies" (see Mooney and Lee 1999) that evoke passionate responses because they involve the clash of deeply rooted principles that kindle an intense public response:

> With little technical information and with high salience, citizen involvement will be increased in all phases, from paying more attention to the debate, to having informed opinions, to actually speaking out and participating actively in the policymaking process (Mooney 1999, 676).

Consequently, decisions to support and oppose the death penalty are often based on moralistic value judgments that are reinforced by opinionated claimants and shallow news coverage rather than practical or factual inquiry (Mooney and Lee 1999; Zeisel and Gallup 1989).

CLAIMS-MAKING AND MEDIA TECHNOLOGY: DEBATING POLITICS IN CYBERSPACE

So what does any of this have to do with the Internet? Matthew A. Baum and Tim Groeling (2008) argue that online technology exacerbates the partisan filtering found in mass media; this includes not only mainstream news websites, but also independent outlets that often operate as "echo chambers, repeating—albeit perhaps magnifying—the 'relatively uniform political content' of the traditional news media" (346).[9] Whether or not this constitutes a trend toward media "bias" that favors conservative ideas in some instances (most notably, Fox News and talk radio) and liberal ones in others (such as MSNBC and *The Huffington Post*), it does indicate that political news in cyberspace favors embellished ideological discord constructed via emotional and moral rhetoric that is similar to what can be found in cable television news. In this sort of political-media environment, it is not unusual to see political candidates like Gabriel Gomez call his opponent Ed Markey "pond scum" after he was depicted next to Osama bin Laden in a distasteful campaign during their 2013 Massachusetts senatorial race (Smith 2013). It has also become commonplace for news personalities to make seemingly outrageous personal attacks, such as former Fox News commentator Glenn Beck calling President Obama a racist on the morning show *Fox and Friends*, and Keith Olbermann describing then Massachusetts senator Scott Brown as "an irresponsible, homophobic, racist, reactionary, ex-nude model, tea-bagging supporter of violence against women, and against politicians with whom he disagrees" during a 2011 episode of MSNBC's *Countdown*. If the Internet is indeed becoming an echo chamber whereby people can go online and simply regenerate the arguments and claims that they obtain via the press and other associations (Baum and Groeling 2008), then we may find that cyberspace does not necessarily foster intellectual political dialogue and debate, but rather mirrors the trend toward partisanship seen in the press.

Zizi Papacharissi (2004) finds that online discussions in politically themed newsgroups actually tend to be civil and polite, noting that users routinely acknowledge and respect differing viewpoints. However, in other cyber-arenas, such as blogs, the prevailing mantra is open partisanship along shared ideological beliefs, which means that bloggers are often speaking to readers who share an interest in, and a perspective on, many of the same issues. Blogging communities, therefore, tend to develop around shared interests and experiences, thereby cultivating highly one-sided debates that can become decidedly less civil and polite as bloggers advance claims related to polarizing issues (Maratea 2008). Furthermore, many social media and mainstream news sites allow users to submit feedback in direct response to published news reports, posts, and tweets; these interactions are often reduced to emotional, moral, and anecdotal accounts that can trend toward being outwardly disrespectful. If you have ever posted your thoughts on Facebook or simply perused what other people have written, then you are probably well aware that the level of incivility in cyberspace can be staggering.

Regardless of whether Internet communication is polite or downright nasty, there are critical intersections between cyber- and offline realities that become particularly salient when people that communicate in emergent online discourse cycles become de facto members of a collective audience whose interactions provide insight into the types of arguments and evidence used to make sense of political issues. What this basically means is that there is fluidity between our offline and online existence: "Logging onto the Internet has become an everyday activity where real world experience informs the perspectives expressed in virtual settings, and vice versa" (Maratea and Kavanaugh 2012, 105). When you internalize news and opinions, they inform how you discuss or debate those issues in cyber-settings, which in turn reflect back on how you think about them once you log off the Internet. It therefore stands to reason that situating yourself in highly partisan online environments can yield an imbalanced understanding of politics that serves to reinforce what you want to believe is right without the hassle of having to genuinely consider oppositional facts. Although Internet communication is somewhat impersonal, in that geographically remote individuals can associate with others based on mutual interest without ever making face-to-face contact, cyber-arenas may nonetheless support interactions that "create symbols of group membership" (Collins 1981, 984).

To understand this point, think about people that converse online about professional sports. These conversations reflect a belief or value shared by the participants, namely an interest in a particular sporting activity or team that may cultivate a powerful bond with considerable emotional investment, which may accrue or diminish in much the same way as occurs in real world environments (e.g., when we win or lose an argument; when others support our assertions; when we are belittled for our opinions, and so forth). In other words, it is possible to experience a level of intensity through online communication that is comparable to what is experienced during face-to-face exchanges despite the lack of direct physical contact with other persons, so long as those interactions are interpreted as meaningful. When sportswriter Martin Manley chose to publish a website that explains the reasoning behind his decision to commit suicide, he did so knowing that observers could use his posthumous Internet presence to better understand his thought processes, study why people end their own lives, and even help those in need cope with the loss of a loved one. While Manley's tale is undoubtedly tragic, his cyber-legacy is a strong reminder that the Internet is a medium capable of transmitting messages with intense passion and analytic profundity. Perhaps this makes it all the more vexing that such potential for depth often remains untapped by the mainstream news agencies that set cultural agendas and influence how we communicate about current events. Although it might be unbeknownst to us as we interact with others, quite often our opinions reproduce the popular dialogues generated by the press and help validate interpretations we simply *know* are correct even though they fail to accurately contextualize political, cultural, and social life (Altheide 2002; Berns 2009; Monahan 2010).

The reality is that news workers, politicians, celebrities, and other powerful public figures are the forces that manipulate our perceptions of political matters both in cyberspace and real-world settings. If the Internet does function as an echo chamber that exacerbates the prevalence of truthiness and anti-intellectualism already rampant in mainstream news cycles, then public discourse may continue to foster narratives that discourage factual understanding of complex social issues. Regardless of whether the outcome is indeed reflective of a "smart idiot" effect, claimants seeking to win our support seem well positioned to continue benefiting from the spread of ideo-logical false-truths that form moral and emotional connections with like-minded thinkers even if they are completely devoid of reality. While it is easy to comprehend how such a media environment can benefit public offi-cials, activists, news workers, and other formidable claims-makers, we are left to wonder whether the information we acquire online is really all that different from what we receive on TV, in a newspaper, or when listening to the radio. It may be that most of us simply do not take advantage of the vast information diversity that exists in cyberspace; or it could be that the ability to interact in relative anonymity and without the same fear of consequence as in face-to-face settings, makes cyber-arenas particularly fertile venues for truthiness to proliferate, irrespective of the intellectual capacity of individual participants. Either way, we may want to heed Stephen Colbert's warning and be mindful of personal and popular perceptions of political affairs being guided by those that "feel the truth" because they "know with their heart" rather than "think with their head" (Colbert 2005).

NOTES

1. Joseph Klapper (1960) conceptualized the idea that mass communication can reinforce existing predilections in three ways. First, people selectively expose themselves to information that coincides with their own values and beliefs (and, as such, ignore content that challenges their worldview). Second, there can be selective perception of materials that violate a person's ideological framework, which means that "regardless of exposure to communication, an indi-vidual's *perception* of a certain event, issue, person, or place could be influenced by his/her latent beliefs, attitudes, wants, needs, or other factors" (Melkote and Steeves 2001, 110). Finally, selective retention means that people can recollect or ignore information based on their own values, perceptions, or dispositions regardless of how the information they consumed was framed. Klapper argues that taken together, these three factors leave people vulnerable to persuasive communication because they selectively receive, process, and interpret the informa-tion, thereby allowing mass media to function as "agents of reinforcement" (see Melkote and Steeves 2001, 110).

2. None of these examples even take into account the popularity of partisan political talk radio programs where inflammatory rhetoric is commonly disseminated to listeners.

3. For the complete poll results, see Cassino, Daniel and Peter Wooley. 2011. "Some News Leaves People Knowing Less." Fairleigh Dickinson University's Public Mind Poll, November 21. http://publicmind.fdu.edu/2011/knowless/final.pdf.

4. See also Karl Popper's critique of positive verification: Popper, Karl R. 1962. *Conjec-ture and Refutations: The Growth of Scientific Knowledge*. New York: Basic Books.

5. See also Ellsworth and Gross (1994); Lord, Ross and Lepper (1979); Roberts (1984).

6. Research conducted by the Congressional Research Service has found that there have been 78 public mass shootings since 1983, a slightly higher figure than the tally reported by *Mother Jones* (Bjelopera et al. 2013). The Congressional Research Service provides non-partisan policy and legal analysis for the United States Congress.

7. It should be noted that these figures only reflect public mass shootings and do not include cult killings, terrorist acts, genocidal-type massacres, and drug- or gang-related homi-cides (Bjelopera et al. 2013).

8. Marshall specifically wrote in *Furman v. Georgia* (408 US 238) that the death penalty is "no more effective a deterrent than life imprisonment, that convicted murderers are rarely executed," that people do not support "purposeless vengeance" on moralistic grounds, and that

the "great mass of citizens would conclude…that the death penalty is immoral and therefore unconstitutional" if they genuinely understand the nature and consequences of capital punishment.

9. Baum and Groeling (2008) also note that wire news sources tend to rely more on traditional newsgathering standards in reporting stories. We may also presume that professional news agencies engage in varying degrees of partisanship, meaning some outlets are more likely than others to frame politics according along ideological lines.

II

Emergent Political Claims-Making

Chapter Three

Power to the People?
Citizen Journalism in Cyberspace

Chances are that you have some sort of experience with social networking in cyberspace—either you connect with friends on Facebook, tweet your latest whereabouts on Twitter, or perhaps you even communicate visually using a webcam. At the very least, you undoubtedly have an e-mail account that allows you to send and receive correspondence electronically. It was not long ago that such modes of communication were unheard of, and the best you could hope for was to catch your friends on the other end of a telephone (land line, of course). The Internet has most certainly changed all of that. Now we can communicate with all of our *virtual* friends with the posting of a single status update, and we can even hold conversations online that defy the barriers of time and place that restrict more traditional forms of communication.

In our day-to-day lives we might not stop to consider the scope of the Internet when we are sending an e-mail, paying a bill, or reading a news report. Yet online technology is so potent that one click of a mouse can result in instantly sharing information with people anywhere on the globe. There is the story of a German teenager who sent out invitations to her 16th birthday party via Facebook but inadvertently neglected to enable a privacy setting and ended up having thousands of would-be partygoers attend. As the *New York Daily News* reported: "The mistake began when the birthday girl . . . published an invitation meant to invite only a few friends over to her house. Instead, 15,000 people checked that they would be there—and her parents promptly cancelled the party. Despite the party-pooper parents, more than 1,500 guests and 100 police officers showed up at the party" (Mandell 2011). In response, CBS News described Facebook as "a powerful tool to invite a lot of people who *aren't* your friends" (Leibowitz 2011, emphasis in original). This is not even an isolated case. A teen in Hertfordshire, England, made a similar mistake on Facebook and accidentally invited over 21,000 guests to her own birthday party (Jamieson 2010). For good or bad, the Internet puts the control of a truly *mass* medium in the hands of ordinary citizens.

If ill-fated online birthday invites tell us anything, it is that everybody with an online connection can interact with almost anyone—known and un-known—in a way that simply did not exist prior to the advent of the Internet. Long gone are the days of the rotary telephone, when real-time long distance communication required each party to be in a particular place at the same time so that their words could be transmitted to each other over the phone lines. Nowadays we communicate wirelessly, whether by cell phone, tweet, instant messaging, live video blog, text message, or any other method of your choosing, almost all virtually free of charge (minus the cost for computer equipment and Internet service). In many ways this has been a very inspiring development for the average person. While most of us might only use the Internet to stay connected with friends and family or to manage our daily affairs, online technology has nonetheless expanded the possibilities for interpersonal communication in ways that were unimaginable in the not too distant past.

Historically, a select group of very powerful people—politicians, news workers, and the like—has controlled the public flow of information in soci-ety. Aside from getting an op-ed published in the local newspaper, most folks have largely been passive consumers of news presented to them by corporate mainstream media agencies. The press largely determines what we perceive as culturally important on any given day, including the political issues that dominate the headlines. In other words, professional journalists function as a cultural filter: The issues, events, people, and claims that news workers ig-nore are unlikely to be perceived as important by the general public.

THE CHANGING NATURE OF *MASS* MEDIA IN CYBERSPACE

When a gunman opened fire in a crowded Aurora, Colorado, theater during a midnight screening of *The Dark Knight Rises* on July 20, 2012, every major news organization was quick to report the details of the crime and speculate on the possible reasons why something so tragic could happen for no readily apparent reason. Yet the story was already unfolding online: Victims' final tweets and Facebook posts chronicled the moments immediately before the shooting; cell phone videos taken inside the theater offered glimpses of the carnage; and survivors delivered real-time updates from the scene. Sites like Reddit—a social news portal where users post content and vote on the most important news stories—provided a minute-by-minute timeline of events, responding so quickly that readers were actually notified when local and national news channels finally began publishing online their first stories about the shooting.

In many ways, the user-generated subject matter presented on Reddit reflects a fundamental transformation in the ways that citizens are able to access public information and exposes the egalitarian potential for news production in cyberspace. While much of what we identify as citizen journalism can be understood as a type of "meta-journalism," or the commenting on, reinterpretation, and reposting of news stories, Luke Goode (2009) has identified an important distinction that emerges when amateurs function as "content creators" (1290):

> The production of news routinely implies a complex and multilayered chain of communication and sense-making: events, issues and ideas will be subject to the influence of various "filters" or "gatekeepers" (sources, journalists, sub-editors) before reaching the public destination. What blogging, citizen journalism and social news sites yield are new possibilities for citizen participation at various points along those chains of sense-making that shape news—not only new possibilities for citizens to "break" news (1291).

The point is really quite simple: The press has effectively lost control of news content because the Internet allows regular people to freely post information and make a vast array of claims void of any mainstream media oversight. For example, when blogger Russ Kick posted photographs of coffins containing the bodies of soldiers killed in Iraq and Afghanistan, and of the *Columbia* space shuttle astronauts, that had been banned by the U.S. government on his website in 2004, the story gained national attention within two days (Grossman 2004).[1] The power to receive the photos, publish them online, and receive widespread mainstream media coverage so quickly speaks to the changing nature of gatekeeping and the ability for average citizens to affect news cycles.

None of this is to say that the press no longer exerts considerable influence over the flow of knowledge in our daily lives; rather, the sheer expanse of cyberspace and its availability to a larger public has fundamentally altered how we acquire and receive that information. Running a simple keyword search using Google or any other online search engine can produce millions of results, ranging from serious news reports to pornographic websites. Most likely you rarely ever need to peruse past the first few pages, meaning the vast majority of websites—and, consequently, most of what is published online—remain otherwise unknown to you. Furthermore, corporations, activist groups, politicians, and the like, can manipulate search results to their benefit, as British Petroleum did following the devastating 2010 Gulf of Mexico oil spill:

BP, the very company responsible for the oil spill that is already the worst in U.S. history, has purchased several phrases on search engines such as Google and Yahoo so that the first result that shows up directs information seekers to the company's official website. A simple Google search of "oil spill" turns up several thousand news results, but the first link, highlighted at the very top of the page, is from BP. "Learn more about how BP is helping," the links tagline reads (Friedman 2010).

All of this suggests that the power to publish does not necessarily correspond to successful reception by consumers, nor does it put laypersons on equal footing with those social institutions that have historically controlled the flow of information in society.

CITIZEN JOURNALISM AND BLOGGING IN A NEW MEDIA WORLD

Given the right circumstances, however, citizen journalists have shown that they can influence mainstream news and political agendas—most notably through the work of bloggers and the availability online of video footage taken with cell phones and other digital devices. Amateurs are not saddled by the rigid deadlines and editorial restrictions that burden professional journalists; they can effectively stay ahead of the media curve by making posts available in real time and constantly updating their sites with additional material throughout the day. To contextualize the speed at which information flows in cyberspace, consider that a video depicting the decapitation of Nicholas Berg, an American in Iraq, by Islamic terrorists in 2004, was downloaded more than 500,000 times within 24 hours of being posted on the web site Consumption Junction (Harmon 2004, A12). We may suspect that most people initially learned of the Nicholas Berg story by watching a news broadcast or reading a newspaper (in print or online). The Internet then allowed them to peruse alternative websites in order to quickly and easily view the unedited video, from which the press censored the most graphic images.

Citizen involvement has also helped make public several important news stories in recent years, including the solicitation of sex in an airport men's bathroom by Idaho Senator Larry Craig, exposing the fraudulent rape charges against Duke University lacrosse players, and the sending of sexually explicit e-mail messages to adolescent boys by Florida congressman Mark Foley. The Foley scandal is particularly noteworthy because news workers knew of his e-mailing teenagers who had served as congressional pages for almost a year before the story broke. It was not until an anonymous blogger posted copies of Foley's e-mail exchanges online in September 2006, that journalists at ABC News finally published the story on its website (Kornblut, Seelye, and Kirkpatrick 2006). In this instance, it was a citizen journalist that prompted a mainstream media response; but it did not become a national scandal until the press began covering the story.

The Larry Craig, Mark Foley, and Duke lacrosse stories exemplify how citizen journalists occasionally out-scoop news agencies, or, at least, how the investigative work done by amateurs sometimes exceeds the efforts made by professional reporters. Bloggers, in particular, have played a prominent role in publicizing a number of important political issues, including the torture perpetrated by American soldiers at Abu Ghraib prison in Iraq, the federal government's inadequate response to Hurricane Katrina, and the Swift Boat Veterans for Truth claims that John Kerry distorted his military record and disparaged the efforts of soldiers, which contributed to his defeat during the 2004 presidential election. As these examples suggest, political claims emanating from the blogosphere—and cyberspace, more generally—are often ideologically charged, highly partisan in nature, and crystallize around specific scandalous events that are cited as evidence of larger social and political problems needing redress.

THE "RATHERGATE" SCANDAL AND POLITICAL CLAIMS-MAKING IN THE BLOGOSPHERE

You may recall that Dan Rather ended his twenty-four-year reign as lead anchor of the CBS Evening News in 2005, having served the longest tenure of any national news anchor in American television history. The events leading up to Rather's retirement marked a seminal moment when the presumed democratizing effect of citizen journalism was most clearly realized. The *Rathergate* scandal, as it came to be known, erupted following a September 8, 2004, report by Rather on "60 Minutes II" questioning the legitimacy of President George W. Bush's military service. Based on the acquisition of four memos that were supposedly written between 1972 and 1973 by Lieutenant Colonel Jerry B. Killian, Bush's commanding officer in the Alabama Air National Guard, the report claimed that Bush was excused from participating in mandatory drills, given higher marks on his yearly evaluation than he had earned, and suspended from flying following his refusal to abide by orders and submit to a physical examination (Seelye and Blumenthal 2004).

The decision by CBS News to air the Killian memos drew the ire of conservative political bloggers, many of whom accused Rather of trying to undermine Bush's campaign during the fiercely contested 2004 presidential election. Since Killian had died in 1984 and the source of the documents was not disclosed by Rather during his report, speculation that the memoranda were fraudulent began to spread rapidly online; skeptical bloggers published their initial claims challenging the authenticity of the memos nineteen minutes into the original broadcast (Pein 2005). Most notably, the blog Little

Green Footballs played a central role in mobilizing the blogosphere by posting "do-it-yourself" experiments that involved replicating the Killian memos using Microsoft Word and then comparing them to digitized versions of the originals in order to show the files had been produced on a computer.[2] Despite this, initial mainstream news reporting of the incident never addressed concerns over the validity of the Killian memos. *The New York Times*, for example, noted that White House communications director Don Bartlett called the release of the files politically motivated, but never actually disputed their authenticity (Seelye and Blumenthal 2004). It was not until Killian's immediate family expressed alarm and document experts were unable to validate the letters as authentic that traditional journalists began questioning the credibility of the original CBS account. Although bloggers broke the story, it was the press that cultivated the scandal by bringing it to the attention of the larger public.

The controversy surrounding the Killian memos largely centered around three types of evidence. First, there were questions about whether a typewriter from the early 1970s could have produced the typography on the documents. Second, the files were said to contain improper military terminology. Finally, those who personally knew Killian were not convinced that he had written the letters presented in the CBS report (Pein 2005). As these concerns became galvanized on a national level, both conservative and liberal political bloggers co-opted *Rathergate* as a vehicle for promoting competing claims of media bias. For right-wing blogs, the scandal demonstrated the prevalence of liberalism in mainstream media reporting; an inability, or unwillingness of the traditional press to effectively verify the accuracy of their reporting; and an overt attempt by CBS News to spoil President Bush's reelection bid. The right-wing blog *Power Line* went so far as to proclaim that *Rathergate* dispelled the myth that "concern for their reputation in the marketplace, and even more among their peers, would prevent [news agencies] from spreading outright falsehoods" (Hinderaker 2004). Leftist bloggers, on the other hand, claimed that "the CBS/document story is . . . proof that there is no goddamn liberal media" (Black 2005). They argued that the incident reflected a double-standard: Dan Rather was vilified for allegedly inaccurate reporting while ample evidence that President Bush failed to fulfill his military obligations was overlooked.

Whereas liberal bloggers did not necessarily dispute that Rather had let "partisanship cloud his judgment" (Black 2005), the press framed the matter as an "embarrassing blunder by duped CBS journalists" who failed to verify the authenticity of the documents in their rush to broadcast the story (Safire 2004b, A23). *The New York Times* condemned Rather for exhibiting poor investigative standards and described CBS News as the "victim of a whopping journalistic hoax" by a begrudged former National Guard officer who supplied the fake documents in hopes of "besmearing a president to bring him down" (Safire 2004a, A23). Officials at CBS responded by conducting an internal inquiry, which concluded that the Killian memos report was aired in haste out of fear that a rival network would beat them to the story (Glater 2005). Several CBS News executives subsequently resigned their positions at the network and Rather abruptly stepped down as the anchor of CBS Evening News.

This outcome was all the more remarkable considering that the story itself had materialized online, which leads us to consider why these particular political claims succeeded in attracting media interest and public attention. Presumably it helped that the burgeoning scandal centered on a media icon like Dan Rather, whose report and use of the alleged Killian memos occurred during a presidential election season. By piggybacking their claims on compelling real-world events, bloggers injected importance to their assertions that CBS News exhibited liberal media bias by airing fraudulent documents with the intent of undermining a sitting President. Although media bias is itself an abstract concept that is difficult to quantify, the Killian memos in combination with the "do-it-yourself" experiments that were validated as legitimate by forensic document experts provided a tangible example with the "appearance of common sense and plain truth . . . and an image of technical expertise" (Hilgartner and Bosk 1988, 61).

According to Stephen Hilgartner and Charles L. Bosk, advancing claims in this manner increases the probability of success: Certified "facts" stated with vivid, emotional, and succinct rhetoric that are combined into "slick, little packages that crisply present issues in authoritative and urgent tones" (62) are well suited for the reporting style of the press. Yet there are undoubtedly elements of randomness and timing that determine why certain claims become socially relevant at particular moments in time. In *Rathergate*, bloggers tapped into the appropriate politically motivated issue at the proper juncture and presented it in a way that was evocative enough to demand the attention of news workers. As Table 3.1 shows, *The New York Times* responded quickly, publishing 37 articles about Rathergate within the first month after bloggers had posted their initial claims about the Killian documents. That interest, however, only lasted for a short period of time; the number of news articles related to the scandal dropped dramatically after the first few weeks.

The decline in mainstream reporting of Rathergate in subsequent months suggests that either the bloggers' claims became too repetitive or the dramatic character of the scandal itself simply diminished in value (Hilgartner and Bosk 1988). This may be attributed to the fact that powerful political interests who were initially implicated in the scandal had no reason to keep the story alive. Reporting on the Killian memos pressured the White House to respond to the allegations that President Bush had not adequately fulfilled his military service, while questions surrounding their authenticity then com-

Table 3.1. Distribution of articles and blog entries about Rathergate for *The New York Times* and select web logs (September 8, 2004–February 28, 2005).

Date	The New York Times	Eschaton (Liberal)	Instapundit (Libertarian)	Power Line (Conservative)
Sept 2004	37	31	138	107
Oct 2004	0	0	6	5
Nov 2004	4	2	22	10
Dec 2004	0	0	7	4
Jan 2005	12	4	27	27
Feb 2005	3	3	6	5
TOTAL	56	40	206	158

pelled John Kerry and the Democratic Party to refute allegations that they had conspired in the documents' release. Since Rathergate forced both political factions to defend themselves against potentially damaging accusations during an election year, its continued presence as a national issue served no constructive purpose for either Republicans or Democrats. Nonetheless, the persistent hounding of conservative bloggers in subsequent months—particularly surrounding the delayed reporting of findings from an internal investigation at CBS—perhaps helped keep the story alive long enough to pressure CBS into forcing the resignation of several news executives, and likely played a role in Rather's ultimate retirement.

While the Rathergate scandal has come to represent a crystallizing moment when political claims generated in cyberspace helped reshape the social, political, and media landscape, it is unclear—and perhaps unlikely—that such an outcome would have been possible if traditional journalists had not breathed life into the story. Although bloggers were indeed successful in having their claims regarding the Killian memos picked up by news agencies, they ultimately had little influence over how those claims were subsequently re-framed, including which individuals or groups were principally credited for discovering the discrepancies in the documents: Mainstream media coverage tended to credit the forensic experts with detecting the forgeries and afforded only an ancillary mention to the work done by bloggers. All of this suggests the emergence of an important paradox. Cyberspace provides an important venue for citizen journalists to produce political claims that may, under the right circumstances, influence news coverage; yet amateur claims-making that occurs online remains wholly dependent on the mainstream press to achieve the requisite public attention needed to merit cultural and political value.

CHALLENGING SOCIAL AND POLITICAL POWER IN CYBERSPACE

If Rathergate teaches us anything, challenging existing power structures in cyberspace is possible, but the process by which it is accomplished might not be all that revolutionary because news media continue to function as an "institutional regulator" (Hirsch 1972, 643) that filters out unsuccessful political claims from those that receive broader consideration. Sociologist Todd Gitlin (1980) makes this point in writing about the New Left student movement that emerged during the Vietnam War. What began as a series of college campus protests to oppose U.S. military involvement eventually became an important symbol of anti-war activism once national media focus propelled the Students for a Democratic Society (SDS) into the political spotlight.[3]

> For their different reasons, the media and the movement needed each other. The media needed stories, preferring the dramatic; the movement needed publicity for recruitment, for support, and for political effect. Each could be useful to the other; each had effects, intended and unintended, on the other (Gitlin 1980, 24).

This relationship is no less symbiotic today. Claims-makers provide media outlets with evocative storylines and dramatic visual imagery, while news agencies direct public attention to citizen journalists and other political activists. So, it may be true that the Internet is giving more people than ever before a public voice, but it is still very much the press that determines which of those voices is newsworthy and meaningful.

Media *sponsorship* is therefore a key element to successful citizen journalism, especially among those individuals with relatively little social capital at their disposal. During the 2011 Arab spring, for example, anti-government revolts in Egypt were documented using cellphone cameras and shared via social media:

> Al-Jazeera's citizen media service Sharek received about 1,000 cameraphone videos during the Egyptian uprising against Hosni Mubarak. Riyaad Minty, its head of social media said: "Post Egypt, in places like Libya, Yemen and Syria, citizens posting online have been the primary lens through which people have been able to see what is happening on the ground. Now our main stories are driven by images captured by citizens on the street, it's no longer just a supporting image. In most cases citizens capture the breaking news moments first. The Arab spring was really the tipping point when it all came together" (Batty 2011).

Despite the best attempts of the Egyptian government to stop the protesters from going online to organize and communicate —which included a five-day blackout of all Internet service in the country—the messages and images continued to flow, offering the outside world a real-time glimpse from inside the uprising. In the aftermath of the insurrection, NBC News correspondent Richard Engel even tweeted the picture of an Egyptian demonstrator holding a sign that supposedly read "thank you Facebook."[4]

Ironically enough, it was Engel that emerged as one of the more vocal critics of the idea that the revolution in Egypt and larger Arab Spring throughout the Middle East was caused by either the Internet or social media. In an appearance on the *Rachel Maddow Show*, Engel stated that the protests "are starting for a variety of reasons, but mostly they are starting because people have had enough," and that he had "been listening to a lot of analysts and have been plugged in over this. Keep talking about Twitter and Facebook. This didn't have anything to do with Twitter and Facebook. This had to do with people's dignity, people's pride. People are not able to feed their families" (MSNBC 2011). More recently, Engel also questioned the value of the Arab Spring when Egypt seems no more stable and democratized than prior to the uprising in 2011, writing, "the days of the protesters with laptops and BlackBerrys in Tahrir Square are long gone" (Engel 2012).

Engel's point of contention as it relates to the Arab spring and Egypt is an important one: To what degree are shifts in social and political power achieved through street-level and online activism maintained over time after protests have ended, claimants been forgotten, and media attention shifted to other concerns? Manuel Castells (2009) describes citizen journalism and other forms of Internet-based interactions as mass self-communication because they are "characterized by the capacity of sending messages from many to many in real time or chosen time, and with the possibility of using point-to-point communication, narrowcasting or broadcasting, depending on the purpose and characteristics of the intended communication practice" (55). Quite simply, this means that computer-mediated communication can be processed instantly or at the user's discretion, respond immediately to changing data, and be simultaneously directed toward specific parties or broader audiences.

Castells suggests that for social change to be realized, the most motivated persons or groups must successfully communicate their message in a way that fosters mobilized resistance through a shared sense of discontent (347). If you think about protesters holding a rally on a street corner, then you can visualize the localized nature of their prospective audience; interpersonal activism is time and place specific. Now, imagine that a local news crew filmed the protesters for a segment on the evening news. Mass media coverage has extended the reach of their claims beyond those who were physically present at the rally. People watching the newscast can draw an interpretation about the protesters' efforts based on how reporters frame the event. If a national network takes notice, the potential audience grows even larger, perhaps even globally if international outlets pick up the story. Although the protest event itself was time and place specific, the possibility of mobilizing support from distant locales increases the more news agencies broadcast the narrative to a broader populace (that is, assuming the press reports on the protest long enough for onlookers to even notice). The necessity of mass media, therefore, exists in its ability to diffuse information across a collective, be it for those in power seeking to maintain the status quo or activists hoping to stimulate social change.

Citizen journalism has shown that collective challenges to social and political authority can be generated en masse thanks to the rapid flow of information that passes through cyberspace.

> The notion of real time is of the essence in this case. It means that people can construct instant networks of communication which, by building on what they do in their everyday lives, can propagate information, feelings, and calls to arms in a multimodal and interactive manner. The message can be a powerful image, or a song, or a text, or a word. The image can be retrieved instantaneously by recording the despicable behavior of those in positions of power. A short SMS or a video uploaded to YouTube can touch a nerve in the sensitivity of certain people or society at large by referring to the broader context of distrust and humiliation in which many people live. And in the world of networked mass communication, one message from one messenger can reach out to thousands, and potentially hundreds of thousands, through the mechanism of the "small world" effect: networks of networks exponentially increasing their connectivity (Castells 2009, 347–48).

The "small world" effect really speaks to the way that information diffusion can snowball online: Citizen journalists post claims to disparate audiences in remote locations across the world, which are then published on other blogs and websites, tweeted—and re-tweeted—on Twitter, splashed across social media, and, in those instances of ultimate success, carried to off-line audiences by news organizations. Don Peat (2010) of the *Toronto Sun* goes so far as to draw comparison to the spread of a virus, where "the average Joe is now a walking eye on the world, a citizen journalist, able to take a photo, add a caption and a short story and upload it to the Internet for all their friends, and usually everyone else, to see."

Of course, posting a picture, video, or petition to a website or Facebook page may constitute a form of civic participation, but socially consequential political claims-making usually requires a broader audience that extends beyond cyberspace. Citizen journalists seeking to truly challenge existing power structures and command public interest must operate in symbiosis with the popular press. In recent years, news outlets have become more responsive to amateur created content, with several network and cable news broadcasters now allowing individuals to upload their own videos in a manner similar to

YouTube and share them online. In some instances a sampling of these contributions is shared on air: MSNBC often scrolls on screen the tweets made by policymakers and private citizens, and cable news anchors sometimes read audience feedback submitted via e-mail, text, and social media during broadcasts. Amidst the 2012 presidential campaign, ABC News and Facebook even collaborated for an interactive Republican primary debate, which included an online application that allowed Facebook users to deliberate on political issues. In speaking about this new model of interactive debate coverage, ABC News president David Westin proclaimed that "discussions and reactions by Facebook members will play into how ABC News approaches its coverage of campaign events" (ABC News 2007).

The idea that citizen perspectives determine political news coverage and inspire punditry seemingly affirms the notion that digital technology is democratizing mass media and the public sphere. However, online interactivity tends to disproportionally exclude economically poor and socially disenfranchised individuals who are less likely to have either a high-speed Internet connection or the requisite free time to be debating political matters in cyberspace. Still, the Pew Research Center has found that 60 percent of American adults use social networking sites, and approximately two-thirds of them engage in some form of political activity using social media (Rainie et al. 2012). Additionally, CNET reports that Facebook members posted about 35,000 messages in a three-hour period during the East Coast broadcast of a 2008 presidential debate. According to those figures, the average person would have had to refresh their web browser 1,750 times in order to read every post—and this would not have included any of the Facebook users responding from the West Coast (Broache 2008). Considering that Facebook now reports having over one billion active users, imagine how many times you would have had to refresh your browser during the 2012 ABC News interactive debate!

With such an extreme surplus of amateur-generated political commentary floating through cyberspace, the likelihood of any one individual being recognized is indeed remote. To this point we have discussed successful citizen journalism as resulting from news organizations reporting on singular events, such as the Rathergate scandal and Arab Spring, which inspired a multitude of political-oriented claims in the blogosphere, on social media, and throughout cyberspace. There are also instances when news agencies adopt specific citizen journalists and publicize their stories to the broader populace. Take the case of Malala Yousafzal, a Pakistani schoolgirl activist who was hired by the BBC in 2009, at the age of eleven, to write a print and online diary about life under Taliban rule. Focusing mostly on a decree that the education of girls be banished as per Sharia law, Yousafzal chronicled her uncertainty of not going to school again if the edict was passed, concerns that the Taliban would raid her school and object to her colorful clothing, and even the tranquility of a vacation where "neither is there any firing nor any fear" of the militant violence that pervaded her everyday life (Yousafzal 2009).[5]

In her most disturbing entry, young Malala describes the chilling paranoia that envelops her existence as a young Pakistani schoolgirl:

> I had a terrible dream yesterday with military helicopters and the Taliban. I have had such dreams since the launch of the military operation in Swat [her hometown of Mingora]. I was afraid of going to school because the Taliban had issued an edict banning all girls from attending schools. Only 11 students attended the class out of 27. The number decreased because of Taliban's edict. On my way home from school I heard a man saying "I will kill you." I hastened my pace and after a while I looked back if the man was still coming behind me. But to my utter relief he was talking on his mobile and must have been threatening someone else over the phone (Yousafzal 2009).

Such stark reality from a young child helped bring global attention to Yousafzal and the plight of women under Islamic fundamentalist reign. By 2011, Yousafzal was nominated for the International Children's Peace Prize and was conferred a National Peace Award (since renamed that National Malala Peace Prize) by the Pakistani government (BBC 2012). Beginning with her BBC-sponsored citizen journalism, the young teenager ultimately became recognized as a symbol of Taliban resistance and an important global voice for female equality.

It also made her a target of Taliban militants. On October 9, 2012, gunman stopped Yousafzal's vehicle as she was returning home from school and proceeded to shoot her in the head and neck for the crime of promoting secularism in Pakistan. Fortunate to survive her injuries, Malala was flown to England for treatment and rehabilitation; her hospital discharge in January of 2013 was noteworthy enough to elicit worldwide news coverage, and her father publicly stated that her ordeal prompted "good wishes of the people across the world of all castes, colour and creed" (BBC 2013). Such a sympathetic response is really quite astonishing considering that a few years earlier Yousafzal was nothing more than an unknown 11-year old asked to write a diary about life as a Pakistani schoolgirl.

CONCLUSION

It may very well be that social reform in Pakistan will never materialize from the saga of Malala Yousafzal and her continued activism. In fact, the outcome is highly improbable. Samira Shackle (2012) writes in the *New Statesman* that the efforts of one girl, however brave, are unlikely to produce profound change when "major politicians and indeed, entire governments, have shied away from making such bold statements against the Taliban."

Yousafzal's tale does exemplify the revolutionary potential of Internet technology: One girl can capture the world's attention and the ire of the Taliban simply by chronicling her everyday experiences. It also makes clear that citizen journalism is not necessarily a truly democratizing form of mass communication. Yousafzal's success (as a citizen journalist), like that of the Rathergate bloggers, is very much the exception to the rule—an outlier—which overshadows the fact that most amateur reporters will never receive any recognition for their work, however groundbreaking or profound. In addition, it is unlikely that the instances of citizen journalism discussed in this chapter would have been recognized as successful had they not been carried to larger and more diverse audiences by the press.

Even with mainstream media validation there remain inescapable problems of authenticity and credibility associated with citizen journalism. Amateur content lacks the formal editorial guidelines of professional news reporting; there are no integrity standards that guide the presentation of information among lay reporters. Bloggers, for example, are often openly partisan, making it difficult to assess the objectivity of claims emanating from these sources. Keep in mind that the press only reported the charges against Dan Rather by conservative bloggers *after* forensic document analysts provided expert corroboration. In today's fast-paced media cycle, fears of being out-scooped can lead correspondents to report on claims made by citizen journalists without thoroughly vetting their sources and content. This not only yields the potential for shoddy news work, but may also undermine the legitimacy of citizen journalism as a reliable source for critical social and political analysis.

The credibility gap is not a concern to be discounted when considering the long-term viability of citizen journalism. The fact that news consumption has been trending away from television broadcasts and print media and toward digital sources accessed via computers and mobile phones does not necessarily correlate to audiences seeking out alternative or independent news sites with greater frequency. Likewise, online users are increasingly being directed toward news stories by family, friends, and peers, but there are no data to suggest that social media affect news choice, and it is likely that posting about political matters on sites like Facebook and Twitter is influenced by mainstream media coverage. Research conducted by the Pew Research Center's Project for Excellence in Journalism has found "that the reputation or brand of a news organization, a very traditional idea, is the most important factor in determining where consumers go for news, and that is even truer on mobile devices than on laptops or desktops" (Mitchell, Rosentiel, and Christian 2012).

These figures may someday change, but the fact that most people tend to frequent larger, trusted news websites may also reflect the credibility gap associated with citizen journalism. Still, cyber-arenas are dynamic and rapidly expanding forms of communication. According to the social media research firm NM Insight (2012), there were approximately 181 million active blogs by year-end 2011, up from 35.7 million in 2006. Certainly not all of them focus on politics and current events, and we may safely presume that many of their authors are not seeking a media platform wider than their immediate social circle. However, this surely leaves a considerable number of bloggers competing for precious public attention. Given that at any moment a plethora of competing claims about a variety of pertinent political matters are being circulated through cyberspace, we must consider whether standards of journalistic integrity can be upheld for amateur reporters. Furthermore, can there be accountability for misleading or falsified reporting when audiences cannot definitively identify the source of the information being presented to them? At present, professional news agencies remain more trusted by audiences than citizen journalists, but it is not clear that their reporting is always more credible. The prevalence of opinion-based programming on cable news has cultivated reporting patterns that are often as opinionated as political blogs. There are also instances when professional news workers sometimes cross the boundaries of journalistic integrity without meaningful consequence. In one notable instance, MSNBC hired Mike Barnacle as an on-air personality not long after he had been fired from *The Boston Globe* for plagiarizing his weekly columns.

Despite these flaws and the overall skepticism that Americans have toward the press, consumers may nonetheless become *more* reliant on Big Media sources in the immediate future to help them identify and summarize the most important stories of the day from the glut of information flowing at all hours throughout cyberspace. Markus Prior (2005) does note that the size of news audiences has been declining for several decades, but that trend might not indicate that people are less interested in political matters: "Changes in available content can affect news consumption and learning *even in the absence of preference change*. People's media use may change in a modified media environment, even if their preferences (or political interest or sense of civic duty) remain constant" (588, emphasis in original). In other words, as the options for where and how we can obtain news have expanded into cyberspace, people have become less dependent on the traditional modes (television, radio, and so forth) of news consumption. This does not necessarily mean that most people are no longer reliant on the press for acquiring political information, but rather they are finding greater media choice. The abundance of available news and entertainment choice on cable television, using digital devices, and when perusing cyberspace makes it easier for people to find content tailored toward their personal interests. Consequently, the vast availability of political claims and information to be found in cyberspace may have a paradoxical affect among people who actually become less knowledgeable about politics because they abandon news and instead focus their attention on preferred entertainment programming (Prior 2005).

All of this makes the prospects for successful citizen journalism even bleaker. Amateurs must first receive mainstream media coverage in order to disperse their claims to a sufficiently large audience. They must then crystallize a civic response from a citizenry whose attention is fragmented across an extensive assortment of news and entertainment alternatives, and maintain that public interest long enough for a groundswell of support to erupt. In truth, the likelihood of achieving each of these goals is rather improbable, making it all the more important to better understand how and why citizen journalists like the Rathergate bloggers succeed in some moments but fail in others. The efforts of activists like Malala Yousafzal are inspiring and not to be trivialized, but we also must consider whether her writing and protest efforts will produce social change if people lose interest in her story and fail to pressure policymakers. Social change often requires a sustained public response that mobilizes political forces into action. It is unclear that any citizen journalist can maintain the necessary media exposure for a long enough period of time to generate a meaningful long-term outcome. At some point in the future, citizen journalists may acquire the political voice needed to revolutionize the public sphere. But until that time, the political power nexus will continue to flow through the press, an institutional blockage that must be overcome if citizen journalism is to ever achieve its democratic ideal as a claims-making vehicle.

NOTES

1. The military had banned the images of service members in coffins, but the blogger, Russ Kick, obtained the photos after filing a Freedom of Information Act (FOIA) request (Grossman 2004).

2. Little Green Footballs established a reputation for being a conservative political blog in the aftermath of the Rathergate scandal. However, the blog's designer, Charles Johnson, described himself in a December 1, 2009, post on the site as an independent who has "bones to pick with both sides."

3. Gitlin (1980) also discusses how mainstream media coverage ultimately contributed to the downfall of the New Left.

4. According to Catharine Smith (2011) of *The Huffington Post*, the Arabic wording on the sign, upon which Facebook was written in English, may actually have read "Thank you youth of Egypt."

5. Yousafzal (2009) notes that the Taliban's interpretation of Sharia is so strict as it pertains to the banning of girls' education, that 150 schools were destroyed in 2008.

Chapter Four

Subverting Old Government with New Media

Understanding the WikiLeaks Effect

When Denver Broncos football player D.J. Williams posted onto his Twitter account a photo of a new iPad given to him by the team in 2012, he unwittingly displayed the power of the Internet to make things that were previously unseen available to the entire world. The problem, for Williams, was that the iPad contained a digital copy of the team's playbook, some of which was visible to anyone who viewed the picture on his Twitter feed. Although Williams quickly deleted the photo, it had already gone viral and spread across the Web to countless sites; information that was intended to be confidential had become firmly entrenched in the public domain. You may find it easy to make light of Williams' gaffe, but the reality is that any of us can have intimate details of our lives published online, whether by choice, by accident, or because someone else shared something about us without our knowledge or consent. Consider the case of a British woman who posted a picture of a dress she intended to sell on the auction site eBay presumably without realizing that she could also be seen naked in the shot. Whether we like it or not, the Internet can take the most private matters and instantly broadcast them to a global public.

The availability of our personal information in cyberspace is in many ways both liberating and insidious. On one hand, the relative anonymity of Internet communication allows us to selectively reveal aspects about ourselves and even develop false personas if we are so inclined. Yet it also makes us more vulnerable to those who seek to do us harm. This is one of the fundamental paradoxes of the Internet age: We can hide our identities more easily in online environments while being increasingly visible to a broader number of people. Perhaps no case exemplifies this dichotomy more than the tragic death of Megan Meier, a Missouri teenager who committed suicide in 2006, following the sudden termination of an online courtship she had via MySpace with a sixteen-year-old boy named Josh Evans. For more than a month, Megan and Josh swapped messages while forging a deeply personal relationship. The tenor of their exchanges abruptly changed when Josh told Megan that he no longer wished to be her friend and began posting disparaging comments about the teen, which concluded with a foreboding final note: "The world would be a better place without you" (Maag 2007). A distraught Megan went to her bedroom closet and hanged herself within twenty minutes of her final correspondence with Josh. The ensuing police investigation revealed that Josh Evans never existed. He was a fabrication concocted by Lori Drew, the mother of Megan's former best friend who later admitted that she adopted the guise of "Josh" to get close to Megan and learn her innermost secrets, which could then be used to publicly humiliate the teen. While the Meier case galvanized public attention to the problem of cyber-bullying and the dangers of adolescent exposure to unregulated online environments, it also shed light on the complex immersion of the public and private spheres that exists in cyberspace.

CYBER-PANOPTICISM AND SELF-SURVEILLANCE IN THE INTERNET AGE

The idea that technology makes us more visible to various forms of surveillance and risk certainly predates the Internet. The assault of Rodney King by Los Angeles police officers in 1992 drew widespread ire after a bystander named George Holliday captured the incident on videotape. Subsequent mass media coverage of the King beating reflects how reproduced imagery remains potent long after the moments when the events themselves occurred (Dennis 2008). The incident also exemplifies the expansive nature of surveillance in modern society. Several decades later, we now have at our disposal a plethora of wireless digital devices that allow us to document the world around us as incidents unfold, often unbeknownst to those being recorded. In Georgia, a substitute teacher was arrested for secretly taking suggestive pictures of high school students who were otherwise unaware that they were being filmed. The instructor was only caught after students perusing Reddit's *Creepshots* online forum recognized their classroom and classmates in the photos (Walsh 2012). In this case, it would seem that technology giveth and taketh away: Digital media allowed the perpetrator to secretly photograph the students; yet his decision to upload the images to the Internet made his crime visible to the viewing public.

In sociological terms, both the King beating and secret filming of adolescents signify the presence of panopticism in an increasingly technological society. Conceptualized by French philosopher Michel Foucault to describe the psychological control over inmate populations achieved through forces of surveillance that are known to exist but are unseen in their operation, panopticism explains how the fear of observation coerces people to modify or control their behaviors. [1]

> Hence, the major effect . . . to induce in the inmate a state of conscious and permanent visibility that assures the automatic functioning of power. So, to arrange things that the surveillance is permanent in its effects, even if discontinuous in its action (Foucault 1975, 201).

Foucault's notion of surveillance is based on the principle that observation has the capacity to alter conduct and enforce discipline based on its perceived effects on the individual, even if it is not perpetually in operation. To better understand what this means, think about walking into a bank and seeing yourself on a monitor that is presumably filming your movements. In that moment, you may become more aware of your actions and take extra precaution to not do anything that might arise suspicion based on your knowledge that you are being watched. Foucault's point is that the power of surveillance coerces us to modify our conduct regardless of whether or not the security cameras in that bank are actually recording.

The extent to which digital technology extends the possibilities and platforms for surveillance means that panopticism has become more expansive in the digital age. It has been well documented that the Patriot Act broadened the federal government's authority to engage in secret intelligence operations on private citizens. More recently, we have learned that the National Security Administration (NSA) is authorized by executive order to monitor the phone calls, e-mails, text messages, and Web browsing patterns of Americans thought to be communicating with parties outside of the United States without having to first acquire a search warrant. Other laws that predate the Internet, such as the Electronic Communications Privacy Act of 1986, facilitate additional surveillance because they do not fully address limitations on government access to modern forms of communication like cell phones and electronic messaging. Online technology, in turn, makes the process of monitoring of citizens' actions much easier to accomplish. In recent years, Google has reported a sharp rise in FBI and other law enforcement requests to access personal e-mail accounts hosted by the provider's *Gmail* service. According to Google's *Transparency Report,* the U.S. government made 7,969 separate demands to examine personal Gmail accounts between January and June of 2012, and these figures fail to include searches of private e-mail accounts hosted by providers other than Google during that time period.

If you think that the implications of government surveillance only affect rank-and-file citizens, then you would be wrong. David Petraeus resigned as CIA director in 2012 after an FBI investigation of his personal e-mails revealed that he had had an extramarital affair. In writing about the Petraeus scandal, *The New York Times* columnist Joe Nocera (2012) disconcertingly notes that "if the most admired military man in a generation can have his e-mail hacked by F.B.I. agents, then none of us are safe in the post-9/11 surveillance machine." These fears of governmental intrusion do not even address the corresponding rise of self-surveillance, or the prevalence with which private citizens monitor and sometimes exploit the actions of other people. Go online and you can probably find videos of famous people like Paris Hilton and former vice presidential candidate John Edwards engaging in a variety pornographic acts; these celebrity "sex tapes" are often unauthorized and reflect the extent to which the Internet can expose our most intimate affairs. It has become relatively common to see events unfold through the lens of amateur videos taken from the scene using cell phones, which are then uploaded to the Internet and sometimes make their way into news reports. The prospect of head-mounted computers with photographic, video, and face recognition technology like Google Glass becoming widely available places our confidentiality at further risk, as does the recent Federal Aviation Administration (FAA) certification of unmanned "drone" aircrafts designed for civilian use: "In just a few years, thousands of commercially operated drones are expected to be doing everything from scientific research to search and rescues, raising privacy concerns among critics, who fear they'll be misused for spying" (DeMarban 2013). There is little doubting the power of modern technology to expose previously hidden aspects of the social order.

WIKILEAKS AND REVERSE PANOPTICISM: MONITORING THE POWERS THAT BE IN CYBERSPACE

Since 2006, the international nonprofit WikiLeaks has used the Internet to publish millions of classified government documents received from anonymous sources around the world. Under the stewardship of editor-in-chief Julian Assange, WikiLeaks is designed to help whistle blowers anonymously disclose important information to the public.[2] Based on the premise that political secrets are more likely to be exposed if sources do not run the risk of being held accountable for leaking confidential documents (Domscheit-Berg 2011), WikiLeaks combines traditional investigative journalism with the radicalism of high-tech hacktivism using computer networks to anonymously promote a political agenda. In many ways, WikiLeaks reflects the changing nature of public discourse in the cyber-age, where open-sourced networks have challenged the institutional authority of political leaders and mass media to exercise control over the flow of information in a way that may prompt "new opportunities for a reshaping of democratic discourse and, potentially at least, of politics itself" (Beckett and Ball 2012, 3).

Micah Sifry (2011) describes the emergence of WikiLeaks as part and parcel of an *age of transparency* engendered by online technology and characterized by greater civic access to information that has been previously been restricted to, and controlled by, the most powerful social and political actors. Using this rationale, proponents of WikiLeaks defend the site as an important guardian of free speech and social justice; a sentiment expressed by Amnesty International in praising WikiLeaks for being a catalyst of the 2010 Arab Spring, which saw popular uprisings against oppressive regimes in countries like Egypt, Libya, Syria, Yemen, and Bahrain. In Tunisia, for example, Wiki-Leaks released documents that chronicled the rampant corruption of then-president Zine el-Abidine Ben Ali, which happened to coincide with news that a young street vendor named Mohamed Bouazizi had set himself ablaze in a suicide protest against the constant harassment of local authorities who demanded bribes before they would issue the required permits for his fruit stand. Although Bouazizi's self-immolation was the crystallizing moment that gave birth to the uprising that would overthrow Ben Ali, the documentation of fraud provided by WikiLeaks allowed journalists to disseminate tales of human rights violations that had previously been unknown or undisclosed: "Leveraging this information, political activists used other new communications tools now easily available on mobile phones and on social networking sites to bring people to the streets to demand accountability" (Walker 2011).

In the United States, WikiLeaks has had a less revolutionary, but nonetheless significant affect on the supposed democratization of citizen access to information in the digital age. WikiLeaks first came to prominence in 2007 after leaking the army's Guantanamo Bay operational procedures; in 2008, messages from Sarah Palin's private e-mail account were published; and in 2009 more than 500,000 pager messages sent during the day of the 9/11 terrorist attacks were posted online. Yet the watershed moment for Wiki-Leaks arrived in 2010, when the now infamous "Collateral Murder" video was made public. The unedited footage depicts three separate Baghdad airstrikes conducted by the U.S. military on July 12, 2007, in which unarmed civilians were killed, including members of the Reuters news service (Bumiller 2010). The disturbing images of the ambush were noteworthy enough to prompt media coverage even though the video's substantive content had been public knowledge since the day of the attack, as indicated by this July 13, 2007, report from *The New York Times*:

> Clashes in a southeastern neighborhood here between American Military and Shiite militias on Thursday left at least 16 people dead, including two Reuters

journalists who had driven to the area to cover the turbulence . . . The two
Reuters staff members, both of them Iraqis, were killed when troops on an
American helicopter shot into the area where the two had gotten out of their
car . . . The American military said in a statement . . . that 11 people had been
killed: nine insurgents and two civilians (Rubin 2007).

The video called into question the military's version of events by revealing
that more people had been harmed than originally claimed; the actual casualties totaled 12 slain civilians and two additional children that were seriously
injured. It also showed that civilians are killed in long-range strikes simply
because they are in the vicinity of the intended target.

OVERCOMING INSTITUTIONAL BACKLASH

Military officials subsequently questioned the credibility of the WikiLeaks
video, claiming that it had been selectively edited to not show one insurgent
carrying a rocket-propelled grenade launcher and another holding an assault
rifle (Fishel 2010). Critics further contended that WikiLeaks had exhibited
unethical journalistic standards by manipulating the footage in an attempt to
distribute anti-war propaganda. Interestingly enough, it was satirist Stephen
Colbert who most forcefully called Assange to task for engaging in political
activism under the guise of whistle blowing during an April 12, 2010, interview on *The Colbert Report*:

Colbert: The Army described [the video] as a group that gave resistance
during the fight. That doesn't seem to be happening. But, there are armed
men in the group. They did find a rocket-propelled grenade among the
group. The Reuters photographers who were regrettably killed were not
identified as photographers. And, you have edited this tape, and you have
given it a title called "Collateral Murder." That's not leaking, that's a pure
editorial.

Assange: So, the promise we make to our sources is that not only will we
defend them through every means that we have available—technological,
and legally, and politically—but we will try and get the maximum possible political impact for the materials that they give to us.

Colbert: So, collateral murder is to get political impact?

Assange: Yes, absolutely. And our promise to the public is that we will
release the full source material. So, if people have a different opinion, the
full material is there for them to analyze and assess.

Colbert: Actually, then, I admire that. I admire someone who is willing to put collateral murder on the first thing people see, knowing that they probably won't look at the rest of it. That way you properly manipulated the audience into the emotional state you want before something goes on the air, because that is an emotional manipulation. What you're about to see is collateral murder, now look at this completely objective bit of footage that you're about to show. That's journalism I can get behind.

Assange: That's true. Only one in ten people did actually look at the full footage.

Colbert: So that's ninety percent of the people accept the definition of collateral murder.

Assange: Yes.

Colbert: Congratulations.[3]

Perhaps more than anything, the Colbert interview shows that WikiLeaks and Assange in particular had attained tremendous authority to define for audiences what constitutes free speech, and how the public should interpret leaked materials.

To some degree, we may question whether the power to selectively frame government and corporate actions comes into conflict with WikiLeaks' stated objective of combining "high-send security technologies with journalism and ethical principles . . . to get the unvarnished truth out to the public" (see http://wikileaks.org/About.html). While some detractors have charged that WikiLeaks has political motives that trump its presumed journalistic mission, others have condemned publishing millions of secret documents as threatening to global, national, and individual security. These fears were manifested when WikiLeaks published sensitive internal U.S. military "war logs" that revealed top-secret information about civilian and friendly-fire casualties in Afghanistan, as well as details about Taliban and al-Qaeda operations, because those documents contained the names, phone numbers, and GPS coordinates of key military informants: "Neither WikiLeaks nor the mainstream news organizations possessed the resources to redact 91,000 documents manually for harm minimization—and while the newspapers might have been willing to go without publishing source material, WikiLeaks emphatically was not" (Beckett and Ball 2012, 52–53).

Although WikiLeaks eventually agreed to withhold many of the Afghan war logs until they could be properly redacted, the incident nonetheless highlighted the risks of rapidly disseminating large amounts of intelligence in cyberspace without the proper capacity to vet those materials. These anxieties were magnified in 2010 when WikiLeaks released over 250,000 classified U.S. diplomatic cables, in what *The New York Times* described as "an unprecedented look at back-room bargaining by embassies around the world, brutally candid views of foreign leaders and frank assessments of nuclear and terrorist threats" (Shane and Lehren 2010). Anger in political circles over the leak generated a scathing institutional response out of fear that the cables would damage America's diplomatic credibility and general standing around the world (Heisbourg 2011). Sarah Palin wrote that the person responsible for the leak should be "hunted down" for being anti-American (Siddique and Weaver 2010), while Senate Republican leader Mitch McConnell and Vice President Joe Biden both labeled Julian Assange a "high-tech" terrorist who should be prosecuted for damaging America's relationship with its allies and placing the lives of key personnel at risk (CBS News 2010a; MacAskill 2010). Former Arkansas governor Mike Huckabee then upped the ante, stating that WikiLeaks' informant should be found guilty of treason and executed (Siddique and Weaver 2010).

Still, Huckabee's pleas for the death penalty paled in comparison to the statement issued by Tom Flanagan, a senior advisor to then-Canadian prime minister, Stephen Harper:

> I think Assange should be assassinated, actually. I think Obama should put out a contract and maybe use a drone or something . . . I wouldn't feel unhappy if Assange does disappear (Siddique and Weaver 2010).

In some ways Flanagan was not far off; Assange was already being investigated for the rape of two women. Facing extradition to Sweden on those criminal charges, Assange managed to avoid arrest when he was granted political asylum by Ecuador in 2012, allowing him to seek refuge in that country's London embassy. Although the move let Assange continue as WikiLeaks' chief editor, the rape charges and his subsequent confinement—he faces arrest and deportation should he step foot outside the embassy—undermined the organization's reputation because media attention was redirected away from the journalistic efforts of WikiLeaks and toward Assange's alleged criminal conduct.

As news narratives began to focus on politicians calling WikiLeaks a cyber-terrorist organization and Julian Assange's personal conduct, public sentiment started to reflect the damage inflicted by these attacks. Opinion polls suggest that the majority of Americans believe the release of diplomatic cables harmed U.S. international relations; most respondents also indicate that the public has no right to know national security secrets; and nearly 60 percent support charging Julian Assange with a crime for releasing the cables (CBS News 2010b; Chaiken 2010). It is particularly salient to note that only 33 percent of those ages 18–29, who are likely to be more Internet savvy than older Americans, believe that publishing the diplomatic memos served the public interest, according to a 2010 Washington Post-ABC News poll (Chaiken 2010).

ANONYMOUS ALLIES AND ASSOCIATING WITH HACKTIVISTS

Of course, WikiLeaks did have vocal supporters that claimed the release of classified materials is protected free speech. Numerous civil rights advocates and watchdog groups also used WikiLeaks as a platform to defend the importance of Internet freedom. One faction in particular, the hacktivist collective called Anonymous, emerged as a prominent cyber-vigilante avenging the perceived injustices perpetrated against WikiLeaks:

> Since releasing the vast cache of diplomatic cables this month, the anti-secrecy group WikiLeaks has been the focus of intense criticism for divulging classified materials, embarrassing the U.S. government and potentially endangering lives. But it has also engendered the frenzied support of an expanding and loosely defined global collective that seems intent on speaking out—and in some cases waging war on WikiLeaks' behalf. The most prominent of those groups is known as Anonymous, which . . . sought to disable the Web sites of several U.S. companies as part of what is called Operation Payback (Shapira and Warrick 2010).

Anonymous' ire was mainly directed at corporations like Visa, MasterCard, PayPal, Bank of America, and Amazon, which either provide online server space but refused to host the WikiLeaks site or froze donations to WikiLeaks by declining to provide payment services (Beckett and Ball 2012; Mackey 2010). At the time of the hacks, WikiLeaks released a statement saying they "neither condemn nor applaud" the attacks, but rather viewed them as "a reflection of public opinion on the actions of the targets" (Pace 2010).

In the wake of Operation Payback, Assange continued to forge critical alliances with hactivist groups. Anonymous, for example, played a conspicuous role finding WikiLeaks needed server space and contributed to the 2012 release of e-mails from the intelligence firm Stratfor: "The Global Intelligence Files represent a far cozier relationship between the two groups, with WikiLeaks actively distributing and promoting the fruits of Anonymous' work" (Greenberg 2012). The publishing of materials that were acquired directly through illegal hacking seemed to fly in the face of earlier claims made by Assange that focused on WikiLeaks' journalistic mission. Yet incidents like Stratfor, the publishing of Sarah Palin's private e-mails, and other similar leaks ultimately placed WikiLeaks in a tricky predicament. Whereas true believers in the fight for Internet freedom may respond favorably to WikiLeaks' relationship with hackers because it increases the potential scope for corporate and government secrets to be revealed, those affiliations are more likely to be frowned upon by the larger, less committal populace.

To the extent that WikiLeaks engages in a journalistic pursuit to uncover truth that is couched in what Christopher Hitchens (2010) describes as a political agenda to undermine governments, generating a sympathetic public response is necessary to remain socially relevant as either a news gathering agency or a credible source for activism. According to a 2010 *Washington Post* report, Anonymous chose to defend WikiLeaks using hacktivist measures because the Internet can help organize the masses into mobilized dissent against oppressive governments, and that the "most important result from doing these attacks is the media exposure" (Shapira and Warrick 2010). Figure 4.1 indicates that there was indeed an increase in mainstream news reports about WikiLeaks *and* Anonymous following the 2010 corporate hacks. This public attention may have benefited Anonymous and its niche core of enigmatic devotees by legitimizing as relevant its form of cyber-dissent. By this time, however, WikiLeaks was seeking a broader mainstream social appeal branded around its charismatic figurehead Julian Assange and its core message of Internet freedom, free speech, and human rights. The problem was that by 2011 there started to emerge myriad reports and commentaries that portrayed Assange as both a victim of government persecution and an egotistical megalomaniac (see Hitchens 2010) who envisions himself as "the James Bond of journalism" through his work as the "founder, philosopher, spokesperson, original coder, organizer, financier, and all the rest" of WikiLeaks (Burns and Somaiya 2010). Under Assange's stewardship, several WikiLeaks volunteers left the organization or were terminated, and critics accused him of exploiting WikiLeaks to pursue his own political agenda against governmental threats to democracy (Burns and Somaiya 2010).

For better or worse, Assange had become the face of WikiLeaks, and his organization was now framed through the prism of an eccentric fugitive attempting to avoid Swedish rape charges and prosecution by American authorities for criminal actions per the 1917 Espionage Act. Even though Assange labeled the accusations against him a smear campaign—and by all accounts there are plenty of people that support his cause—the persistent negative press coverage that resulted from news agencies reporting on his attempts to avoid extradition and U.S. politicians calling for his apprehension only served to draw his most vocal support from hactivist groups like Anonymous, who themselves could easily be cast as extremists with harmful social intentions. While this in itself may have been sufficient to cultivate negative perceptions about Assange and WikiLeaks from average citizens, it is helpful to revisit the praise that WikiLeaks received from human rights groups for its role in rousing public opposition to oppressive regimes throughout the Middle East during the Arab Spring. Hailed for releasing documents that provided previously unknown insight into how badly the governments in those

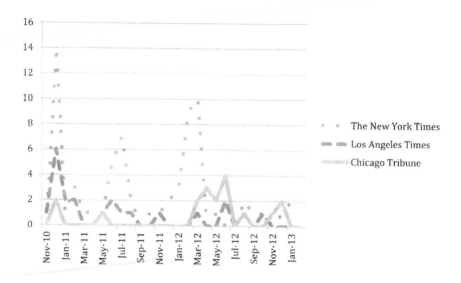

Figure 4.1. News Articles Mentioning WikiLeaks and Anonymous Published by Month on Select Mainstream Media Websites, November 2010 to February 2013

countries were repressing their people, the degree to which WikiLeaks actually served as a catalyst for uprisings that had likely been bubbling underneath the surface for several decades is debatable. Yet the adoration is nonetheless notable in comparison to the responses we have seen in Westernized nations, where active institutional mobilization against WikiLeaks and Assange has helped produce anything but revolutionary outcomes.

SEEKING MEDIA SUPPORT

Regardless of whether you consider WikiLeaks a journalistic organization or simply a mechanism for political activism, its viability in either capacity is fundamentally tied to news agencies framing its operations as credible and summarizing the content of leaked documents for the larger populace that lacks the time, energy, desire, or knowledge to sift through all of them. From the time of it origins, WikiLeaks had over one million documents ready to be processed and then posted online (Domscheit-Berg 2011). According to Craig Silverman (2010) in the *Columbia Journalism Review*, it was logistically impossible for WikiLeaks' staff on its own to fact-check and determine the authenticity of every document prior to their being published. Consequently, a symbiosis of sorts emerged between the group and several major news agencies needed to authenticate their data:

WikiLeaks opened up a trove of documents on the Web, while the three news organizations that had been granted early access to the documents coordinated their own release schedule and then published their own takes. Some of what was uncovered in the documents was already known or reported, but the breadth and depth of the information gave new weight and urgency to the debate over the war. In one sense, the carefully choreographed exercise represented a new kind of hybrid journalism. WikiLeaks was more than just a source, it was a publisher. And however it got the goods, WikiLeaks found willing collaborators in the mainstream eager to both compete on a big story and to serve their readers (Silverman 2010).

The news outlets selected by WikiLeaks to screen the war logs, diplomatic cables, and other documents—namely *The New York Times* in the U.S. and *The Guardian* in England—were more than receptive to the opportunity for breaking such potentially newsworthy scoops. This partnership not only brought mainstream media attention to WikiLeaks, it also validated the importance of the information contained in the leaked materials: "If WikiLeaks had released the documents on its own, the initial debate and coverage would have focused on whether the material was real, thus delaying any discussion about the contents. By enabling a process of distributed verification, Assange was able to ensure the conversation about the documents moved immediately to the information they contained, not whether they were authentic" (Silverman 2010).

These collaborations proved to be a powerful source of political strength for WikiLeaks. Allowing journalists to function as fact-checkers responsible for sifting through the trove of documents assured that the most politically salacious details would be reported to the public. Of particular importance, the decision to outsource verification of the war logs and diplomatic cables let news workers censor the materials and minimize any possible risk to individuals that might be identified and harmed by their publication. Assange's subsequent decision to publish uncensored versions of the U.S. diplomatic cables on the WikiLeaks website, however, was met with scorn by the very news firms with whom WikiLeaks had worked to release the redacted files: Assange was swiftly condemned for violating journalistic ethics by failing to protect against the social or personal harms that can result from full disclosure of confidential materials. According to reports in *The Guardian*, Assange presented himself as a supporter of conscientious redaction (*The Guardian* 2011), but also allegedly described the individuals named in the war logs and diplomatic cables as "collaborators" whose fates would be justified by WikiLeaks' pursuit of the greater good (Beckett and Ball 2012, 86).[4]

ASSESSING THE WIKILEAKS EFFECT

The emergence of Julian Assange as the symbolic leader of online "advocacy journalism" and the fight for free speech and institutional transparency in an era of global networking has had tremendous implications on the growth and legitimacy of alternative, radical political media in cyberspace. His strategic use of new media technology has allowed WikiLeaks to sidestep traditional avenues for public relations, which typically involve using hired staff to communicate with supporters and creating press releases or other materials that can be used by news workers to spread the word to larger audiences. By harnessing the power of the Internet, an otherwise innocuous group of underground activists has been so successful at infiltrating and exposing the highest levels of governmental and corporate secrecy that it compelled mainstream news organizations to develop working collaborations with WikiLeaks. If public responses to WikiLeaks are any indication, then the group has been wildly successful in achieving social relevance by advancing novel forms of journalistic-based cyber-activism that traverse the boundary separating political protest from professional news gathering. In many ways, WikiLeaks has rewritten the playbook on networked political activism because it does not simply direct newsworthy claims toward journalists; it has made that information publically available on a mass scale and *worked in partnership* with the press in order to reach even broader audiences and maximize the group's political impact.

It is important to understand that it is not unprecedented to see the press functioning in tandem with activists. Students during the Vietnam War, for example, would often notify news agencies in advance of campus protests to ensure that reporters would be present to film footage of draft cards being burned. Yet the widespread recognition that WikiLeaks has attained using tactics that do not involve visible, physical public protest reflects the changing nature of advocacy and journalism in an online world. The fact that WikiLeaks is still available to audiences despite its refugee Chief Editor being confined to the Ecuadorian embassy in London and numerous governments trying to block access or bring down the site is a powerful reminder that networked cyber-activism can be incorporated across numerous countries using a complex structural model that protects the location of online servers, storage spaces where the electronic documents are filed, and the methods for collecting the donations needed to fund WikiLeaks (see Whalen and Crawford 2010).

It is perhaps ironic that the intricate process of operating WikiLeaks necessarily lacks transparency in order to thwart cyber, legal, and governmental attacks against the site, and protect donors' identities and monetary contributions. That a relatively small journalistic outfit run by upstart activists could establish operational hubs across the globe in order to securely collect and distribute sensitive materials on a cyber-network that exists outside the jurisdiction of any one bureaucratic or legal entity is reflective of an emergent model of political claims-making that could not exist prior to the Internet. While this is an important development, it is unclear whether the WikiLeaks model will be more widely adopted by other advocacy groups. Most political activists avoid protest tactics that can be framed as treasonous because their long-term viability is predicated on the ability to mobilize the support of allies and resources needed to subsidize their social movement or claims-making campaign, as well as rebut the criticisms of opponents attempting to undermine their credibility. In addition, shifting media focus on Assange's burgeoning celebrity, intense institutional backlash, news coverage that framed WikiLeaks as aligning with extremist hackers, an increasing sense of desperation attached to antics like the planting a faux news story on *The New York Times* website, and the declining novelty attached to leaking documents that had no earth shattering effect all likely contributed to diminishing public sentiment. Poll data now indicate that 60 percent of Americans believe that WikiLeaks' efforts have harmed U.S. national security, and more than half of respondents view Bradley Manning— the source of the largest set of leaked documents published on WikiLeaks—as a traitor (Rasmussen Reports 2013).[5] Although WikiLeaks remains in operation, it has periodically had to shut down its website due to funding shortfalls (Whalen and Crawford 201), and the group reported receiving donations of €32,838 to cover expenses exceeding €246,619 in the first half of 2012 (Wau-Holland-Stiftung 2012).

For all its hype, we may ask whether WikiLeaks has had a truly transcendent effect on American politics. There is no denying that the Internet offers claimants the unique ability to concurrently infiltrate the backrooms of political insiders, communicate directly with constituents, and disseminate claims to a global audience. Yet as WikiLeaks reveals, the dynamism of online technology does not alter the underlying reality of political activism: Claims become irrelevant if people stop listening to them and their messenger. This is not unlike the publishing online of a sex offender registry. It is publically available and contains important information, but its relevance diminishes significantly if most people do not bother to check the names on the list. WikiLeaks continues to post leaked documents online that presumably expose government and corporate secrets. But the damage inflicted by the institutional attacks against WikiLeaks, the shift in media storylines toward the tale of Julian Assange, the group's involvement with hackers, and the general information overload produced by the sheer volume of leaked material have all contributed to thwarting the promising potential of WikiLeaks as a cyber-arena for networked advocacy journalism. The Internet, then, provides new ways to spread the word, but does not make those claims inherently worthy of public sympathy if the claims-makers themselves are discredited and unable to remain socially relevant.

To clarify these points, we can draw a useful comparison between Wiki-Leaks and the release of the Pentagon Papers, which were classified documents that chronicle U.S. involvement in Vietnam from 1945 to 1967. The contents of the Pentagon Papers were leaked to *The New York Times* and first published in 1971: "They demonstrated, among other things, that the Johnson Administration had systematically lied, not only to the public but also the Congress, about a subject of transcendent national interest and significance" (Apple 1996, E5). The files were so controversial that their release prompted the Nixon administration to charge journalists at *The New York Times* under the 1917 Espionage Act and order the newspaper to cease further publication of the documents (Frankel 1996). *The Times* would eventually appeal the injunction in *New York Times Co. v. United States* (403 U.S. 713), where the Supreme Court ruled that a free press is necessary to expose government corruption.

With this precedent in mind, the parallels between WikiLeaks and the release of the Pentagon Papers suggest that the Internet supplies activists with a new way of doing old things on a much grander scale. The growing mass of documents on WikiLeaks is so large that few people—and perhaps no media organization—have the time or desire to sift through all of them, and none of the leaks published by WikiLeaks have proven to be as consequential as the Pentagon Papers. Supporters may argue that WikiLeaks helped cultivate the Arab Spring, but this would require accepting that Julian Assange posting some PDF documents online was the crystallizing event that boiled over citizen anger, which had been percolating over the course of several decades. While this is possible, it is not necessarily plausible, especially given that Mohamed Bouazizi's self-immolation in Tunisia precipitated the nationwide revolt against President Zine el-Abidine Ben Ali and fostered the subsequent uprisings in Egypt and across the Middle East.

In many regards, the evolution of WikiLeaks validates the continuing importance of sympathetic mainstream media coverage for advocacy journalists and all sorts of political claims-makers. The more recent revelation of NSA warrantless wiretapping that came to light due to the whistle-blowing efforts of Edward Snowden, the former NSA analyst who revealed himself as the source of the leak in hopes of exposing "the dangerous truth behind the U.S. policies that seek to develop secret, irresistible powers and concentrate them in the hands of an unaccountable few" (Gellman and Markon 2013). Unlike Bradley Manning, the majority of Americans view Snowden as a "whistle blower," and his exposé preceded a major public opinion shift (Brown 2013), with 53 percent of Gallup respondents disapproving of government surveillance programs (Newport 2013). In a separate Quinnipiac University poll, 45 percent of voters believe that anti-terrorism measures go too far in restricting civil liberties, a considerable change from 2010, when only 25 percent said that such measures were overzealous (Brown 2013). Whether or not this swing in public perception will remain stable in the future is unclear, especially considering that media coverage of Snowden has decreased dramatically in recent months. While there is still a scattering of reports on Snowden, much of his story has become tabloidized by tales of his GED-level education, pole dancing girlfriend, and even a marriage proposal from infamous ex-Russian spy Anna Chapman. Of course, the dominant storyline has been Snowden's fleeing the United States to avoid espionage charges; first traveling to Hong Kong and then spending more than one month in the international transit section of a Moscow airport before being granted temporary asylum.

For his efforts, Snowden became a fugitive. Presently living somewhere in Russia, he has virtually disappeared from American news cycles, doomed—at least for the time being—to the state of insignificance that envelops claims-makers that are no longer sufficiently newsworthy.[6] Shifts in media coverage toward the institutional attacks levied against WikiLeaks and the enigmatic Assange's eccentric, if not criminal, behavior similarly reflect what seems to be the declining cultural significance of WikiLeaks. In truth, by 2011 WikiLeaks had saturated the market with a multitude of documents that had impactful but short-lived newsworthiness. Once reporting on the collateral murder video, the Afghan war logs, the diplomatic cables, and any other relevant leaks had run their course, they were largely forgotten— lost in the abyss of irrelevance as public attention shifted to other important matters, like the banning of large sodas in New York and the latest Kardashian affairs. When WikiLeaks had first made available one million previously confidential documents, there was an inherent novelty to their efforts; news agencies were more than willing to verify the contents because the size and scope of the leaks, and the information that might be contained therein, was unprecedented.

Fast-forward several years and the growing quantity of documents on WikiLeaks has seemingly become old news, so to speak. Politicians and corporate leaders rarely if ever have to answer for the information that continues to be exposed by WikiLeaks. It would seem that quantity does not necessarily equal quality. For this reason, the WikiLeaks effect does not compare with similar pre-Internet investigative exposés like the release of the Pentagon Papers and the break of the Watergate scandal, which led to the resignation of President Richard Nixon. It is possible that WikiLeaks will achieve similar success in the future, but it may have to regain some of its cultural luster. To the degree that WikiLeaks remains unable to take ownership of its own identity in news media and popular culture, the group will persist in being defined, in part, by institutional critics and as an extension of Julian Assange. While the Internet may indeed be an important vehicle for transmitting claims, we may suspect that these types of narratives will continue to undermine the legitimacy of WikiLeaks regardless of how many documents are published online.

NOTES

1. The notion of panopticism actually has its origins in the work of Jeremy Bentham, whose Panopticon prison design maximizes staff surveillance by ensuring that inmates can always be observed, but will never actually know when or if guards are watching them. For more, see Bentham, Jeremy. (1787) 1995. *The Panopticon Writings*, edited by Miran Bozovic. London: Verso.

2. On its website, WikiLeaks describes its mission as follows: "Our goal is to bring important news and information to the public. We provide an innovative, secure and anonymous way for sources to leak information to our journalists . . . Publishing improves transparency, and this transparency creates a better society for all people. Better scrutiny leads to reduced corruption and stronger democracies in all society's institutions, including government, corporations and other organisations. A healthy, vibrant and inquisitive journalistic media plays a vital role in achieving these goals. We are part of that media."

3. Full video of Assange's interview is made available by Comedy Central and can be accessed at http://www.colbertnation.com/the-colbert-report-videos/270712/april-12-2010/julian-assange.

4. See also Leigh, David and Luke Harding. 2011. *WikiLeaks: Inside Julian Assange's War on Secrecy*. New York: PublicAffairs.

5. Bradley Manning was sentenced to 35 years in prison with the possibility for parole after eight years, and given a dishonorable discharge from the U.S. Army for violating the Espionage Act of 1917 due to his role in supplying classified government documents to WikiLeaks. Since his conviction he has sought to undergo sex-reassignment therapy/surgery and changed his name to Chelsea Elizabeth Manning.

6. Kimberly Nordyke noted in a *Hollywood Reporter* article on July 17, 2013, that Glenn Greenwald, the investigative reporter who broke the Snowden story, secured a book deal to tell the story of Edward Snowden and secret government surveillance programs.

III

Institutionalized Political Claims-Making

Chapter Five

Connecting the Web to the Street

Hybrid Social Movements and Online Advocacy Networks

Imagine that you are a political activist with lots of motivation but few resources. In the past, you would probably have had an exceedingly difficult time coordinating and paying for the mass correspondence needed to spread your message. Even if you were successful, the effort would likely have drained your finances without any guarantee that your labors would bring attention to your cause. How might the ability to communicate globally—not just to thousands of people, but billions—for a comparably cheap price make your political protest more accessible to average citizens? In theory, at least, the Internet may be leveling the playing field by removing (or, at least, reducing) the traditional barriers that have blocked entry into political claims-making, allowing even the most fledgling activists to assemble cost-effective social networks, mobilize resources, and coordinate protest action.

Historically, the biggest obstacle faced by most political activists is that they are *outsiders* who must overcome tremendous adversity if they are to be successful in their claims-making endeavors. We commonly identify social movement organizations, nonprofits, and interest groups as outsiders because they typically lack sufficient social and economic might and have a hard time getting people to listen to their claims. To better understand this idea of outsider activism, think about the public protests that ensued in 2010 after Scott Walker, the newly elected Governor of Wisconsin, proposed legislation to severely weaken that state's public employee unions. Thousands of concerned teachers, firefighters, police officers, and other state workers, along with their supporters, stormed the Wisconsin statehouse in hopes of defeating the bill. Each of those protesters had very little social power individually;

collectively, however, they helped shape the national discourse pertaining to workers' rights and the value of labor unions. Over the past several decades, unions have suffered sharp declines in clout and membership: approximately 36 percent of public sector and 7 percent of private sector employees belong to a union; this amounts to just under 12 percent of the total workforce (Bureau of Labor Statistics 2011). In the immediate aftermath of the protests, however, numerous opinion polls showed a considerable increase in public support for unions, and fourteen Democratic state senators even fled to Illinois in order to prevent the bill from being ratified (Saad 2011).

Yet for all their successes, the Wisconsin protesters failed to achieve their ultimate goal. Walker eventually signed the anti-union legislation into law and, unable to maintain media interest in the story, public attention gradually shifted to other more newsworthy events. This is the fundamental dilemma faced by outsiders: They lack a persistently authoritative social voice that compels government officials to take action. As a result, they are forced to obtain (and maintain) sufficient media attention to raise public awareness to their claims. The problem, however, is that there is only so much air-time and print space that news agencies can dedicate to reporting on current events and political concerns. Consequently, there is intense competition among outsiders for media coverage, which is not only difficult to obtain, but often can be fleeting for activists whose message fails to remain relevant (Hilgartner and Bosk 1988).

Absent sufficient entrée into both media and government, outsiders have historically relied on grassroots, attention-grabbing, street-level forms of public protest. Riots, marches, rallies, and sit-ins are the types of actions taken by outsiders to gain notoriety in hopes of rectifying problematic social conditions. Joel Best (2008) notes that "activists hope that these activities will lead to media coverage, and that attracting publicity to their cause will bring their claims to the attention of the public, so that, in turn, both the media and the public will press policymakers into action" (64). Of course, simply getting recognized by the press does not guarantee that outsiders will garner a receptive public response. Take the Westboro Baptist Church, whose members have received scathing social criticism in recent years for picketing the funerals of slain military soldiers and murder victims in protest against society's growing acceptance of homosexuality. You might ask why a group of people would do something so insensitive. The answer is quite simple: recognition and media coverage. While most of us may frown upon the actions taken by the Westboro Baptist Church, they have nonetheless become recognizable for branding a publicity stunt so extreme in nature that it has induced a journalistic response. In truth, the Westboro protesters are the exception and not the rule. Most outsiders are not widely acknowledged for their efforts because their claims fail to resonate with journalists and therefore are never received by the larger audience of news consumers. Staging public demonstrations—even distasteful ones—can be a rather expensive and time-consuming process that requires both a great deal of organization and sufficient financial resources. Many activist groups simply lack the necessary infrastructure and available assets needed to coordinate those types of high-profile events.

ONLINE ADVOCACY NETWORKS AS OPPORTUNITY STRUCTURES

Given that the long-term sustainability of any political movement is dependent on motivating people into collective action, the ability to fashion online networking structures that make it more economically feasible to disseminate claims, communicate with the public, and acquire resources stands to revolutionize how modern social movements operate. Internet technology certainly provides a conduit through which activists can more easily establish contact with supporters from whom needed backing and material assets can be acquired.

> Hundreds of social movement organizations network each other by email lists. Many also have websites and electronic bulletin boards or other conferencing spaces on the Internet where users can directly interact with each other. For social movements, which typically have limited membership and financial resources, the Internet is revolutionizing the rule of the game (Nip 2004, 23).

Because of this, some speculate that the Internet is "influencing the emergence and development of social movements," which, in turn, are being "molded in the image of the Internet" (Clark and Themudo 2006, 51).

Victor W. Perez (2013) suggests that the Internet is helping to reshape outsider activism because it offers a dynamic *opportunity structure* whereby social movements can establish a "digital hub to an elaborate network of interconnected web-spaces, which together [present] a unified front . . . a collaborative effort to control and manipulate information . . . and an electronic vehicle for worldwide claims-making" (76). The term "opportunity structure" simply means that there are external factors that can help legitimize and embolden social movements. Traditionally, activists have benefited from both political and cultural opportunities. Political opportunity structures become available when activists acquire access to power, obtain influential allies, rifts develop among elites, and when alignments shift, such as when a political party gains electoral control or opposition to a social movement becomes weaker (McAdam 1996; Tarrow 1996). Cultural opportunities similarly involve an element of timing:

> The most obvious cultural opportunity is the occurrence of a newsworthy event that focuses attention on a troubling condition . . . They lead to a widespread sense that a particular troubling condition, previously neglected, must now be addressed. Activists who have been struggling to have their claims heard may suddenly find themselves in demand—reporters seek them out for interviews, legislators invite them to testify at hearings, and so on—because they are the ones who understand and have ideas for what to do about the troubling condition that is now the focus of concern (Best 2008, 79–80).

Essentially, cultural developments and political systems can influence activists' ability to successfully advance their claims by structuring their prospects for collective action.

Perez suggests that online advocacy networks exist as technological opportunity structures that can facilitate success when favorable cultural or political moments emerge by helping activists communicate claims at times when people are more receptive to hearing them. He also argues that technological opportunities can help social movements remain sustainable in the absence of political and cultural opportunity structures by affording a semblance of public visibility to activists and supporters who "coalesce online into an informal, yet unified collective of claims-making entities dedicated to a mutual cause" (Perez 2013, 88). In particular, Perez identifies five key benefits of online networking. First, the Internet provides "theoretically unlimited space for unrestrained claims-making" (76). The power to publish claims does not in itself guarantee success, but online technology allows activists to sidestep mainstream media gatekeeping and communicate unfiltered information directly to prospective audiences. Second, cyber-networks function as electronic gateways with numerous entry points by which people can access, learn more about, and contribute to a movement; they have high degrees of structural fluidity and can be reshaped by simply adding or removing hyperlinks that connect web spaces to each other. Third, online networks help forge a collective identity and commonality of purpose among supporters of a movement because they facilitate communication among people that may be demographically disparate in real-world settings, thereby "uniting individuals with shared experiences and beliefs and strengthening ties among them" (Perez 2013, 79–80).

The fourth benefit for claimants is the possibility of controlling information using cyber-arenas. This can be tricky because activists cannot necessarily control where audiences choose to peruse online. However, when advocates use the Internet to disseminate claims via "a unified protest network of inter-linked websites" (Perez 2013, 83), they are attempting to manipulate adherents into becoming immersed in a collection of web spaces that espouse similar claims and offer a relatively narrow breadth of information about a given subject. In other words, the more a person utilizes advocacy networks to obtain information about a movement or a cause, the less likely they are to receive divergent perspective about those issues. Finally, claimants can relay engaging tales of lay experience in cyberspace, which personalize their cause, validate their conclusions, and corroborate (or vilify) empirical expertise. Although these accounts may be nonprofessional and anecdotal in nature, they may nonetheless be presented as evidence that confirms claimants' positions and reinforces audience support (Brown 1992, 1997; Perez 2013). To the extent that these benefits allow claimants to cost-effectively challenge the institutional barriers that have traditionally hindered outsider activism by establishing a global communication stream, forging a commonality of purpose among allies that might have otherwise remained disconnected, and providing a buffer to insulate proponents from opposing perspectives, then it stands to reason that online advocacy networks can be an important catalyst to sustain and advance modern social movements.

ORGANIZATIONAL HYBRIDITY AND CONTEMPORARY SOCIAL MOVEMENTS

It is becoming more common for outsiders to incorporate online strategies that focus on networking and communication alongside the coordination of offline operations. When put in practice, this *organizational hybridity* simply means that a growing number of contemporary social movements and interest groups are integrating both online and real-world tactics into their organizational models (Chadwick 2006). Think of this as being like the formation of a smart mob where participants are notified electronically—via e-mail, text message, and so forth—of a time and place to assemble and then gather in a public space to stage some sort of predetermined protest action (Rheingold 2002). While the ultimate success of a smart mob depends on participants' physical performance, electronic media facilitates rapid, on-the-fly communication, which helps coordinate activities so quickly that they sometimes appear to have emerged spontaneously.

Unlike smart mobs, which are time and place specific, social movements have a formal infrastructure, engage in more organized forms of political activism, and require sufficient material resources to sustain operations during periods of malaise. As David S. Meyer (2007) writes, social movements arise through the endeavors of individuals who are unified by a collective sense of purpose and are willing to engage in "sustained efforts that challenge existing or potential laws, policies, norms, or authorities, making use of extraconstitutional as well as institutional political tactics" (10). Provided the right opportunity exists—for example, a newsworthy event that grabs public attention like a school shooting or natural disaster—these activists may suddenly find themselves with an audience of concerned citizens whose growing interest increases the likelihood of gaining access to important pow-

er structures and influential political allies that may otherwise remain unavailable.

THE TEA PARTY AS A HYBRID MOVEMENT

To the extent that outsider political activism is influenced by the existing
social climate, which may encourage or hinder protest action, it is important
to consider how the Internet may supply new opportunity structures to more
effectively organize, network, and rally support. In recent years, the
American Tea Party has emerged as one of the more notable political protest
movements to effectively facilitate online operations that focus on claim
dissemination, recruitment, and resource acquisition with coordinated offline
mobilization. The rise of the Tea Party is particularly interesting given how
the impassioned and seemingly spontaneous protests that defined the movement in its infancy were strategically coordinated in a way that gave the Tea
Party an important competitive advantage in its quest for public exposure and
political relevance. Whereas most fledging outsiders struggle to remain solvent, corporate tycoons have bankrolled the Tea Party from its inception;
their financing allows the movement to sustain an infrastructure that can
support "grassroots" planning and recruitment on a national level (Boykoff
and Laschever 2011). Consequently, cynics speculate that the Tea Party is a
disingenuous *astroturf* movement because its supposed grassroots support is
actually manufactured by corporate interests (see Klotz 2007).[1] These
charges are not without merit. Several national organizations, including the
Tea Party Patriots, Tea Party Express, and Tea Party Nation did emerge in
large part from the strategic organization of high-powered conservative political advocacy groups, such as FreedomWorks and Americans for Prosperity.
The broader Tea Party itself, however, is somewhat of a fragmented movement comprised of local chapters that operate independently but are loosely
affiliated by a shared belief in lower taxes, fiscal responsibility, and limited
federal government (Boykoff and Laschever 2011).

Despite the lack of any formal centralized leadership, the Tea Party rose
to national prominence thanks to a slew of public demonstrations that received considerable news coverage. Much of the early media attention was
focused on the movement's ideological platform and flamboyant public rallies, which were replete with protesters adorned in Revolutionary War era
costumes. The most noteworthy Tea Party events occurred on April 15, 2009,
when "tax day" demonstrations were reportedly held in more than 750 cities
in all 50 states. Additional gatherings continued across the nation, including
the Taxpayer March on Washington on September 12, 2009, which was
organized through the coordinating efforts of the political advocacy group
FreedomWorks and the promotion of Fox News commentator Glenn Beck,

who had "seized on the date—the day after the anniversary of the Sept. 11 attacks—as a symbol of what he called national unity" (Phillips 2009).

In subsequent months, news coverage chronicled the rise of the Tea Party, its ardent supporters, and a string of notable victories in the 2010-midterm elections. While much of the Tea Party's success was credited to the cultural fervor spawned by the public protest rallies—images of which were routinely splashed across news reports—the Tea Party from its inception complemented its public activism with a visible online presence. If you enter the search term "Tea Party" on Google, Yahoo, or any other search engine, you are likely to find that the first few pages of results are mostly comprised of links directing you to prominent national Tea Party organization websites, which generally engage users to "find out more" about the movement and its platform, "take action" with ongoing protest campaigns, and "get connected" with fellow tea partiers throughout the country. Chances are that most people who believe in Tea Party ideals and want to learn more about the movement or become a more active participant will seek out that information online. Although, activists cannot determine where individuals choose to explore the Web, they can attempt to manipulate the outcome to their advantage by creating a multitude of access points from which people can gain entry into their online network and retrieve claims about core issues related to the movement.

All of this is profoundly important because social movements that are unable to cultivate and maintain a motivated and vocal nucleus of support tend to fade into oblivion. Public rallies undoubtedly brought notoriety to the Tea Party and nurtured its growth. The Internet's value to the movement in fostering organizational hybridity has been much more subtle, but equally valuable. The decentralized structure of the Tea Party means that most national, regional, and local affiliate groups operate independently and may not work directly on joint action. However, the Internet enables stronger interconnectedness between these organizations and the larger movement through the creation of an online nexus encompassed around mutual values and the exchange of a shared ideological discourse (Keck and Sikkink 1998). Perez (2013) notes that hyperlinked websites are directly connected, which helps cultivate a working partnership between individual entities within a social movement even if those "sites do not explicitly endorse each other or necessarily accept the information contained on one another's sites" (76). In other words, hyperlinking expands each individual group's ability to carry problem claims beyond the boundaries of their own web spaces, while also serving as a funneling mechanism that directs users to other areas of the Internet that are congenial to their aims, goals, and values.

The use of hyperlinks thus creates a digital networking structure through which claimants may try to obtain a measure of control over where audiences go to acquire information by encapsulating them in a self-contained bubble replete with sympathetic content, claims, and websites. Within the Tea Party cyber-network there is a sort of structural fluidity that is neither firmly hierarchical nor rigid in nature, meaning that its shape may fluctuate based on the addition or removal of affiliated web spaces, a person's initial or primary entry point, and whatever additional sites they choose to explore (see Figure 5.1). Whereas websites for prominent national organizations are likely to be more visited than others—high-profile groups like the Tea Party Express will generally get more web traffic than local chapters—hyperlinked connections establish a multitude of gateways from which people can navigate to the sites of different groups allied with the Tea Party. As importantly, online networking serves as a conduit for individual organizations within a larger movement to present themselves as a unified front capable of advertising claims, disparaging critics, and encouraging protest action without having to organize additional public demonstrations or obtain news media attention (Perez 2013).

For modern outsiders, the use of cyber-arenas make it easier to communicate with supporters, reinforce a commonality of purpose, control the dissemination of sympathetic claims, and present audience feedback that corroborates the values of a movement, which may indicate that the sustainability of political activism is becoming less reliant on media coverage than has been the case in the past. However, this might not quite be the case—at least not yet. The Tea Party may have burst onto the political scene with corporate-subsidized rallies and the implicit endorsement of Fox News, but there has been a noticeable downswing in the movement's public visibility in recent years. During the 2010 midterm elections, critics suggested that some Tea Party-backed candidates were unfit for office. These claims were magnified when Delaware senate candidate Christine O'Donnell aired a cam-

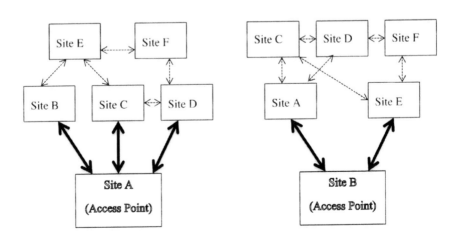

Figure 5.1. Structural Fluidity of Hyperlinking in an Online Advocacy Network

paign ad assuring voters that she is "not a witch," and when Sharron Angle proposed unhappy voters adopt "Second Amendment remedies" during her Nevada senate campaign. In addition, numerous instances of racism were chronicled at Tea Party rallies, including accusations that protesters spat upon Democratic representatives Emanuel Cleaver, John Lewis, and Barney Frank.

Sociologist Todd Gitlin (1980) notes that these sorts of criticisms undermine the credibility of a political movement and tend to gain media traction once activists have become sufficiently newsworthy to establish legitimacy with the general public. As scrutiny of the Tea Party became magnified, there was a coinciding decline in the number of large-scale grassroots rallies that played such an important role in the Tea Party initially attaining social and cultural relevance. Although smaller, localized demonstrations continued in various parts of the country, the movement was eventually co-opted by figureheads that assumed unofficial leadership roles on the national level. Two of the more prominent personalities that emerged were Minnesota Representative Michelle Bachmann, who founded the congressional Tea Party Caucus in 2010, and former vice presidential nominee Sarah Palin, who in the same year headlined a 46-city national tour sponsored by the Tea Party Express. The rise of Bachmann and Palin as prominent Tea Party frontrunners reflected the extent to which insider lobbying and charismatic leadership had displaced the grassroots populism that had originally characterized the Tea Party. Although Tax Day rallies were again held across the country in April of 2010, the press was no longer covering Tea Party demonstrations with the same fervor, and mounting criticism had seemingly started to destabilize the movement.

USING ONLINE NETWORKS TO SUSTAIN THE CULTURAL RELEVANCE OF A HYBRID MOVEMENT

By late 2012, journalist E.J. Dionne declared the Tea Party movement to be dead, writing, "the grand ideological experiment heralded by the rise of the tea party has gained no traction" because "there was no profound ideological conversion of the country" inspired by Tea Party activism. Whereas two years earlier Tea Party-backed candidates swept into office across the country, the 2012 election was a staggering electoral defeat. Dionne argues that ideological extremism—which contributed to the Tea Party's ascension because it provided a lightning rod for supporters to crystallize their feelings of anger and disenfranchisement—has been the primary catalyst in the movement's presumed decline because the vast majority of Americans are otherwise moderate in their political beliefs. Faced with the challenge of remaining culturally relevant, the Tea Party as a collective was forced to make important tactical choices on how best to disseminate claims, continue generating the support of bystander publics, parry the counter-attacks made by political opponents, and shape public policy outcomes (see Benford and Snow 2000). Because the Tea Party is a hybrid movement, it uses a mixture of online and offline tactics to overcome these obstacles; yet its decentralized configuration means that there is no leadership mechanism to consolidate the movement's political clout and provide organizational structure for member organizations and their supporters. Unlike the civil rights movement, which easily attracted media attention because news organizations were drawn to the issue of social justice and the charismatic leadership of Martin Luther King, Jr., the Tea Party has no revolutionary ideas or credible symbolic figures upon which the press can compose sympathetic news narratives. For a time Sarah Palin was somewhat of a media darling, while politicians like Michelle Bachmann and Marco Rubio assumed a leadership positions in Congress. However, political opponents have been reasonably successful as discrediting their efforts. For example, you may recall Rubio getting mocked for his dry mouth, which precipitated "a terrifyingly intimate moment of eye contact with the audience before taking a quick sip from an unfortunately tiny bottle [of water] and then ducking to put it back" during his Republican response to President Obama's 2012 State of the Nation speech (Crouch 2013). Although the response to Rubio's gaffe was tame by comparison to the press's treatment of Palin and Bachmann, the larger point is that journalists have spent as much time scrutinizing congressional Tea Partiers as praising their efforts.

Likewise, civil rights organizers proved adept at staging non-violent demonstrations, such as bus boycotts and marches, that were inherently newsworthy and helped frame social control responses as undeniably racist. Tea Party protests similarly captured the public's attention, but ultimately were unable to sustain media interest for several reasons. As a movement, the Tea Party advocates dissent in the name of civic order, which is not the sort of revolutionary change or sweeping reform that has historically captivated news workers and audiences because it does not really promote social transformation. Furthermore, the ideological principles that fueled the Tea Party were muddled by news imagery that often focused on protesters dressed in farcical costumes and charges of racism, both of which undermined the credibility of the movement. Lacking a strong source of central authority to help frame the movement, dismiss the growing number of increasingly vocal opponents, and manipulate news narratives, organizational efforts that focused on cyber-networking emerged as fundamentally important to the sustenance of the Tea Party.

When the Tea Party began to losing control of its message, it was confronted by a problem that is inevitably faced by all social movements: "People rarely recognize actionable grievances on their own or spontaneously.

Organizers help them do this and direct the efforts of recruits toward an extremely broad range of potential activities, including donating or raising money, working in campaigns, showing up at events, chanting slogans, writing letters, and breaking windows" (Meyer 2007, 61). In its early days these efforts were effectively accomplished through the formation of national and regional activist groups, which provided a real-world organizational platform to collectively express their grievances. Political action committees and corporate interests infused the movement with the cash needed to finance claims-making campaigns, protest events, and political lobbying. News organizations then provided the requisite media attention needed to attract a broad base of supporters by publicizing the rallies that legitimized the movement. These coalitions were facilitated online using advocacy networks that allow individuals to stay actively involved in the movement using their computers, smart phones, and other digital devices.

Interestingly, when the bond that directly connected supporters of the Tea Party movement *on a national level* became predominantly the product of media presentations of symbolic leaders like Sarah Palin (which were increasingly negative) and advocacy networks established in online environments, it may have actually strengthened the attachment between the Tea Party and its most ardent supporters. Shifting news frames that negatively portrayed the Tea Party served as a rallying point that fortified ties among adherents who cast themselves as victims using anecdotal accounts of media bias. For example, visit the Tea Party Command Center website and you can learn about the top-50 examples of liberal media bias, while the Tea Party Patriots (2013) proclaim that the press is guilty of "ideological plagiarism" and "intellectually dishonest hyperbole" for reporting critically on the Tea Party. Anyone choosing to peruse these and most other websites affiliated with the Tea Party advocacy network will presumably be exposed to similarly ostentatious claims, which we may assume coincide with their own lay perspectives if they are supporters of the movement. These assertions of media bias become even more credible when they are validated by "expert" sources, such as when Fox News Channel host Clayton Morris claimed without evidence that "mainstream media [were] casting tea party protesters as violent and racist, the same media that characterized leftist protests against President Bush as patriotic" (Fox News 2010).

There is, of course, considerable irony in Morris's comment, as he appears guilty of espousing ideological favoritism while condemning other news agencies for their alleged bias. Yet it is important to remember that these sorts of statements merely need to resonate as valid among audience members who believe that *news coverage is only prejudiced against their values, beliefs, and ideals*. In this case, we have the corroboration of expert analysis (Morris and Fox News) with anecdotal accounts (the claims presented on Tea Party website) and lay experience (the personal knowledge of Tea

Party adherents) forming a powerful bonding agent whereby "there is potential for their subjective understandings . . . to become 'truth'" (Perez 2013, 85). The broader value of cyber-networking, however, can be understood by its ability to marshal support from bystander publics and keep the movement's ideals relevant in the minds of independent and ambivalent citizens. By facilitating online communication, the Internet establishes social ties among disparate and geographically remote followers who would otherwise have no means of interacting with each other. Their shared beliefs, and the ease with which people can connect with like-minded others, may then help to build and reinforce a communal sense of collective identity among Tea Partiers (see DiMaggio et al. 2001; Nip 2004). While these relationships are vital to the sustenance of a social movement because they represent the formation of *weak* ties that are "indispensible to individuals' . . . integration into communities" because they bind together populations whose interpersonal relations would otherwise be nonexistent or lacking in mutual intensity and intimacy (Granovetter 1973, 1378). Yet these social ties may not be strong enough to draw uncommitted onlookers into the fold or motivate more dedicated supporters into participating in the sort of disruptive real-world protest that has traditionally characterized successful social movements.

Malcolm Gladwell argues this point by noting that the most effective instances of activism occur when people that are closely bonded by shared principles are motivated to take strategic risks in hopes of affecting social change:

> The kind of activism associated with social media isn't at all like this. The platforms of social media are built around weak ties. Twitter is a way of following (or being followed by) people you may never have met. Facebook is a tool for efficiently managing your acquaintances, for keeping up with the people you would not otherwise be able to stay in touch with . . . .This is in many ways a wonderful thing . . . But weak ties seldom lead to high-risk activism (Gladwell 2010).

Gladwell's argument is not that the social ties cultivated in cyberspace are less meaningful to participants than real-world interactions, or that they lack emotional intensity, intimacy, and fail to involve communicative reciprocation (see Granovetter 1973). Anyone who has spent too much time arguing with friends about frivolous things on Facebook or any other social media site knows this all too well. Rather, he is suggesting that online advocacy networks help increase participation because they merely require that people sit at their computer and log on to a website. This, he suggests, does not facilitate the type of responses needed to successfully sustain a movement because it lessens "the level of motivation that participation requires" (Gladwell 2010).

All of this becomes relevant when considering the long-term preservation of hybrid movements. Social networks are fundamental to the process by which people identify the shared norms and values that precede their decisions to engage in collective action (Passy 2003). From this perspective, online advocacy networks provide individuals with a vehicle to establish, cultivate, and reinforce their identification with political causes. To the extent that outsiders must convince prospective supporters to "become personally involved in collective action," the Internet is a profoundly important tool for providing the "opportunities to do so on a sustained basis" (Diani 2003, 7). Yet if cyber-networking fails to cultivate the same sort of *visible* success traditionally garnered through grassroots efforts, then it may intensify feelings of confusion and frustration among those participants who feel like they are doing their part but are failing to produce the results they anticipated. Although activist groups can counter this by publicizing claims that highlight the movement's victories, these feelings may be further exacerbated if the social ties that bond supporters to each other and the movement are weakened by an overreliance on cyber-networking at the expense of trying to attract the requisite media attention needed to remain relevant in the public consciousness.

CONCLUSION

When we think about the Tea Party as a hybrid political movement, the question that has yet to be answered is whether outsider claimants can effectively incorporate online communication networks in a way that will nurture long-term success. Whereas similar campaigns in recent years—most notably the Occupy activists—were unable to sustain themselves after their fleeting grassroots success had dissipated, the Tea Party remains a relevant political entity that continues to draw both the praise of political supporters and consternation of its most outspoken critics. Yet the Tea Party might go the way of Occupy if it is unable to identify new ways to reignite benevolent news coverage and mobilize supporters. Although online technology has engendered important new revenue streams and advocacy networks, an overreliance on the Internet to disseminate claims and communicate with the public could signify that the outsiders' central message may have a more difficult time reaching *not yet* supporters who would be sympathetic to their cause but have not been sufficiently introduced to the movement to compel them to visit them to visit affiliate websites. Similarly, there are no guarantees that cyber-networking can attract sufficient levels of media exposure and public interest for activists to remain solvent minus the visible symbolism of grassroots, street-level protest.

For political claimants the Internet is like a specialty dish at a fine restaurant or a "doorbuster" bargain at a retail store: It is designed to pique your interest and compel you to keep coming back and spending more money in the future. Claims-making, and activism more generally, are essentially forms of advertising. When you visit a Tea Party website, representatives of the movement are selling you on their issues and ideology, its importance, and why *you* should get involved. The claims presented online therefore must resonate in a way that lures people to regularly visit those sites so that they develop a connection to the movement and become sufficiently motivated to donate money and other resources. In the most ideal circumstances, the outcome is not simply the strengthening of collective identity and commonality of purpose among supporters; it is the crystallization of those shared beliefs through mobilized response. For example, you may recall the 2011 London riots that erupted after police in Tottenham, England, fatally shot twenty-nine-year-old Mark Duggan. Protesters who were alleged to be seeking justice for the Duggan family became recognized, in part, for their use of mobile devices and social media like Twitter to organize the insurrection (Halliday 2011; Moore 2011). The "BlackBerry Riots," as they would come to be known, exemplify how "spontaneous" mass protest can emerge, or at least spread quickly, thanks to new media technology

Evgeny Morozov (2011) notes, however, that the Internet is so thoroughly tied to state power that it is not sufficiently liberating as to overcome the shackles of government oppression. In fact, Prime Minister David Cameron at the time of the Duggan protests suggested that rioters be banned from all forms of mobile communication and Internet availability be restricted during periods of civil unrest to prevent mobs from spreading in scope (Halliday 2011; Morris, Wright, and Sherwin 2011). In other areas of the world the Internet is actively banned, censored, or otherwise restricted by bureaucratic forces. This social control element to the Internet (Altheide 2004) comes into direct conflict with arguments that modern communication facilitates the ability to "organize without organizations," as exemplified by the aforementioned smart mobs, Twitter Revolutions, and Blackberry Riots (see Shirky 2008). Part of the problem for activists is that government authorities are aware of the Internet and are capable of acting preemptively to restrict or cut entirely their cyber-communication networks (Morozov 2011).

Wherever the truth may lie, understanding how the Internet is shaping outsider claims-making and activism ultimately requires that we avoid making hyperbolic statements about how new media technology is revolutionizing the social order, or simply dismissing online networking as irrelevant. We know that the Internet enables the formation of communication streams that cost relatively little to operate, reduce the effort required to participate in social movements, and connect previously isolated, uninformed, and even uninspired political supporters. While such developments are important, "there are countless groups upon which the Internet has had little effect, apart from spurring them to establish a simple web page;" and despite the benefits of Internet communication, "many groups and movements have not fundamentally changed their organizations and strategies" (Chadwick 2006, 142). For this reason, projecting how the Internet will affect outsider claims-making in the long run is unclear. Online advocacy networks may have a unifying effect that bonds supporters to an ideology or cause (Perez 2013), but disruptive public actions and sympathetic news coverage are the catalysts that have historically thrust social movements into cultural relevance. In this sense, the Internet may be a devil in disguise for grassroots activists and outsider claimants. The immediate benefits of online technology can be seen in the ability to publicize claims, facilitate communication, control information, acquire resources, and emphasize a common purpose among supporters. However, those advantages may be overshadowed by the inability of online technology to replicate the dramatic, public, and newsworthy forms of protest action that allow outsiders to achieve widespread notoriety. Consequently, Internet technology may ultimately hinder the long-term viability of outsider claims-making if it is not utilized alongside effective grassroots activism.

NOTES

1. The term "astroturf" as it pertains to activism was first coined by former Texas Senator Lloyd Bentsen and refers to campaigns that cloak institutional, political, or corporate sponsorship so as to fraudulently appear grassroots (see Mayer 2007).

Chapter Six

From Back Rooms to Cyber-Lobbies

How the National Rifle Association Uses the Internet to Mobilize Support

In recent years we have been exposed to an ever-growing number of news reports on the prevalence of gun crime and the frightening incidence of mass shootings in the United States. Sociologist Barry Glassner (1999) has found that the number of murder stories on nightly network news broadcasts rose by 600 percent between 1990 and 1998, despite the fact that murder rates actually declined by 20 percent during that time (and these figures are likely tame by comparison to local news coverage). Representations of violent crime in entertainment programing are similarly skewed: Instances of murder and attempted murder account for most of the criminal events depicted on popular crime television programs (Soulliere 2003), despite the fact that murder only accounts for about 1 percent of estimated violent crime (and a mere 0.1 percent of total crime) recorded in the 2011 *Uniform Crime Report.* Notwithstanding these media distortions, there is little debating that gun crime is disproportionately high in the U.S. compared to other westernized nations, and few crimes elicit an enraged public outcry more than a mass shooting.

Whether it is Columbine, Virginia Tech, or someone "going postal," you probably know the storyline all too well. James Holmes opens fire at an Aurora, Colorado, movie theater in July of 2012, killing 12 people and injuring 58 others. More recently was the horrific Sandy Hook elementary school shooting, in which Adam Lanza gunned down his mother, 6 school staff, and 20 young children in Newtown, Connecticut. All told, there have been 62 shooting incidents in the United States that involved 4 or more fatalities since 1982, seven of which occurred during 2012 (Follman, Aronsen, and Pan

2012).[1] Neil Steinberg of the *Chicago Sun-Times* notes that while each of these crimes led to a tragic and regrettable loss of life, the abundance of news coverage dedicated to mass shootings is disproportionately high.

> What mass shootings are is dramatic—deranged gunman bursting into public places murdering innocents for no reason at all. That catches and holds the public's attention, certainly more than random individuals falling off ladders or slipping in bathtubs do, and the truth of the situation—38 percent of the people who die in the United State die from accidents, versus .003 percent who die in mass shootings—does nothing to change the attention the media lavishes on the subject (Steinberg 2013).

Although the number of shooting incidents where the killer's motive appears to be mass murder has risen in recent years (Follman 2013), coverage of these sorts of extreme crimes is prominent in modern news and entertainment media, and the majority of reports put forth gross mischaracterizations of the etiology, extent, and nature of violent crime (Monahan and Maratea 2013; Sacco 2005). David Altheide (2002) attributes this trend in coverage to a prevailing media logic that encourages news workers to present crime using shocking tales and fear-laden storylines that resonate with audiences.

You can be sure that politicians and other political claims-makers are well aware of how the press operates, so they actively seek to connect with citizens by making themselves publically visible on issues like gun control, violent crime, and victimization. It is in those moments—when people are feeling most vulnerable in the aftermath of a particularly heinous crime—that we are bombarded with claims about the causes of such horrible violence and what we must do to recalibrate society's moral order. Often there is no empirical evidence to support the sources of blame and proposed solutions relayed to us by the press. But when we are desperate for solutions, condemning video games, movies, and "shock rockers" like Marilyn Manson, is perhaps more comforting than throwing up our hands and admitting we have no answer. It is precisely this uncertainty that gives claimants a platform upon which they can disseminate compelling claims about the symptoms of violent crime and a whole host of other supposed social ills. Political claims-makers can therefore enhance their probability of success by piggybacking their efforts on dramatic real-world events that redirect media attention to their specific cause and give them access to influential allies that may have previously been unavailable (Ungar 1992). Practically speaking, this means that anti-gun advocates will have an easier time crystallizing public support for gun control legislation immediately following a mass killing than during a period of relative calm.

In the aftermath of particularly infamous school shootings like Columbine and Sandy Hook, it is common to see a plethora of news reports that dissect the possible causes of such terrible crimes and what can be done to prevent horrors like these from happening again in the future. While most people wrestle with how to make sense of these crimes, activists are mobilized into action in hopes of convincing us that they understand the problem and know how to solve it. Take the renewed calls for stronger federal and state regulations on the public availability of firearms and ammunition following Sandy Hook. In Connecticut, the coalition *CT Against Gun Violence* quickly hit the streets to push for "common sense" gun reform, working alongside supporters to promote grassroots advocacy like the March for Change, a rally organized by private citizens that included speeches by state politicians, gun crime victims, and even a survivor from the 2007 mass shooting at Virginia Tech (Shelton 2013). Similar demonstrations were organized around the country by advocates that suddenly had an audience of concerned citizens whose attention had been once again redirected to the issue of gun violence thanks to widespread media coverage of the latest shocking crime.

NOT ALL POLITICAL CLAIMS-MAKERS ARE CREATED EQUAL

If the tale of gun violence was only being told by activists seeking to restrict access to certain firearms and ammunition, then there would likely have been enough cultural fervor to compel legislators to enact sweeping reform. However, counter-claimants inevitably emerge and attempt to discredit their opponents' positions (Best 2008). In response to Sandy Hook, the National Rifle Association (NRA) sprung into action in an effort to stunt the burgeoning momentum of gun control advocates by publically campaigning and lobbying politicians in defense of law-abiding Americans' Second Amendment rights. Established in 1871, the NRA is a nonprofit organization that promotes responsible gun ownership, as well as firearm education and safety training. With membership exceeding 4.5 million people (U.S. Senate 2013), the NRA can flex considerable political and financial muscle to the general public through highly funded ad campaigns and in political backrooms by lobbying policymakers.

According to the Center for Responsible Politics, the NRA spent almost $1.5 million in direct contributions to politicians and more than $25 million in efforts to influence the outcomes of elections between 2011 and 2012. With that kind of economic firepower at its disposal, the NRA has a tremendous advantage over outsider activists and citizen journalists.

> Much of the group's influence stems from a relentless lobbying effort, in Washington and throughout the country, driven by a staff of 80 and a huge and well-organized grass-roots base. In 2012, it spent nearly $81 million on member communication and mailings . . . At the same time, gun control advocacy groups have struggled to match the NRA in finances and influence. The Brady

Campaign spends a little more than $3 million per year (Gold, Tanfani, and Mascaro 2012).

The NRA's fiscal might is in many ways part and parcel of its political clout. Supportive politicians need little more than financial contributions to solidify their patronage of the NRA, and opponents who fear electoral wrath are often swayed to acquiesce on the issue of gun rights, particularly given that they cannot rely on similar funding or voter mobilization from the anti-gun lobby. New York Senator Charles Schumer spoke to this point during a 2012 Senate session when he declared that "the NRA's main strength is because they have two, three, four million people who care passionately about this issue . . . who are mobilized at the drop of a hat . . . [so that we] hear much more from people who are opposed to the assault weapons ban than people who are for it" (C-SPAN 2012). Schumer's comment is not meant to suggest that people who support gun control are less passionate about the issue; rather, they advocate from a disadvantaged position because collectively they have less power that the NRA to influence the legislative process.

In sociological terms, the NRA's potency derives from its *insider* status as a member of the polity, which consists of pressure groups "that can routinely influence government decisions and can ensure that their interests are normally recognized in the decision-making process" (Useem and Zald 1982, 144). Insiders often deal directly with policymakers, giving them sufficient political influence to broker deals and manipulate outcomes without first having to pique social interest by attracting media attention to their claims. Because they are not entirely immune to public opinion, insiders do conduct "clout building" campaigns that are designed to monitor how the larger citizenry responds to their issues and remind legislators of their political sway (Best 2008). However, unlike outsiders that *must* rely on media exposure to raise awareness and mobilize support, pressure groups like the NRA have the ability to *choose* whether it is in their best interest to promote claims discretely behind the scenes or aim for maximum publicity.

Having insider status ultimately allows the NRA to influence legislative outcomes even when there may appear to be little opportunity to do so. Thus, even though you may never see people marching in the street in support of the coal or tobacco industries, you can be sure that the halls of Congress are jam-packed with lobbyists defending their interests, even if they come at great social cost to you and me. The fact that more Americans have historically supported the need for environmental protection over energy production (Newport 2009; Jones 2010; Saad 2013) has not precluded energy sector lobbyists from brokering deals with policymakers that benefit the corporations they represent regardless of ecological risk.[2] The same principles apply to pressure groups like the NRA, which we saw firsthand when Congress struck down a bill proposed by Senators Joe Manchin (WV) and Pat Toomey

(PA) in April of 2013. The legislation would have required private firearm dealers to conduct background checks when peddling to prospective buyers online and at gun shows (Lillis 2013). Although polling data suggest that around 90 percent of Americans support expanded vetting on gun purchases (The Hartford Courant 2013), the NRA exerted its considerable sway and successfully lobbied against the proposed measure, in part, by threatening to mobilize against public officials that voted to restrict gun rights.

Whereas corporate lobbyists derive their power from the economic might of their clients, the NRA can be understood as more of a hybrid pressure group whose extensive teams of lobbyists, lawyers, and public relation specialists do their work out of the public spotlight, but nonetheless draw their legitimacy from the more than four million members that provide substantial political clout. Success for the NRA therefore hinges on compelling those contributors to furnish the financial assets needed to fund claims-making operations and maintain the group's extensive infrastructure. Traditionally, coaxing supporters into championing a cause was accomplished through techniques like cold calling, pamphlet distribution, or public events. The adoption of Internet technology increasingly allows claimants to target prospective audiences in a far more efficient manner by facilitating *perpetual* resource mobilization via online membership drives, fundraising, merchandising, and cyber-protest techniques that can be accomplished with very little time and effort.

UNDERSTANDING CYBER-ARENAS AS A MOBILIZATION STRUCTURE

Andrew Chadwick (2006) adopts the term "e-mobilization" to describe the use of online technology "for political recruitment, organization, and campaigning" (144), and identifies three main areas where the Internet effect has been most visible. First, advocacy groups are using the Internet to complement offline brick-and-mortar operations by developing "new ways to reach out to supporters and the media or put pressure on political elites" (115). Second, transnational (and presumably domestic) protests are increasingly being campaigned in virtual spaces. Finally, novel forms of cyber-protest have emerged that did not exist prior to the Internet and are adopted exclusively in online environments. As we will see in this chapter, e-mobilization has in many ways innovated the process of grassroots political activism by allowing activists to take operations that normally occur offline and shift them to online spaces where they can be accomplished more efficiently and for less cost (Vegh 2003). The ultimate goal is to *link the Web with the street* (see Clark and Themudo 2006) by developing cyber-strategies that (a) cultivate truly meaningful mobilization among supporters and (b) reduce, or even replace, the practical need for attention-grabbing street-level activism, such as public rallies, sit-ins, and marches.

When put into practice, the NRA incorporates e-mobilization by using its websites as venues to publish claims and other information that espouse its agenda, while also disparaging the policies and practices of political opponents that seek to restrict access to firearms and ammunition. These claims are then supplemented by online activism designed to stimulate followers into supplying the symbolic and material resources needed sustain operations and continually build clout among policymakers. Using the Internet in this way generates a useful mobilization structure for pressure groups and all sorts of other political activists because it allows for protest action to be completed while expending little physical effort. All of this is designed to accomplish a very specific goal: Inspire supporters to take some form of action in support of the NRA. If you have ever heard Martin Luther King, Jr.'s famous "I Have a Dream" speech, which he delivered during the 1963 March on Washington for Jobs and Freedom, then you probably recognize how powerful claims can be when they strike a chord with the general public. The images and words from that event resonated so strongly that they placed tremendous pressure on public officials to institute legislative reform, which not coincidentally would happen shortly after with the passage of the Civil Rights Act of 1964 and the Voting Rights Act of 1965.

Cyber-activism may not inspire the same types of dramatic responses as the March on Washington, but it nonetheless has inherent value to pressure groups and other claimants. Although e-mobilization is considerably more docile by comparison to a large-scale grassroots rally, it may compel a broader array of prospective supporters to more consistently participate in mobilized action because those efforts are less time consuming and require little physical exertion. Furthermore, public demonstrations are time and place specific. Online activism, however, allows people to simultaneously fight for gun rights in Connecticut, greater school safety in California, and lower taxes in Washington, D.C., all without leaving the comforts of home. Consequently, it is possible to participate in hundreds, if not thousands of cyber-protests in less time than it would take to attend a single NRA rally.

MOBILIZING SUPPORT FOR GUN RIGHTS IN CYBERSPACE

When news broke of the Sandy Hook elementary school shooting in December of 2012, many people believed that we had reached a tipping point. Transpiring a mere five months after James Holmes had slain 12 people in Colorado and just 14 days after Kansas City Chiefs football player Jovan Belcher killed himself and his girlfriend, the murder of 20 young children led some to suggest that we "look at the results of the tragedy to ensure that this moment leads to a transformational movement" (Martin 2012). While the nation was grappling with how to respond to such a senseless tragedy, and parents questioned the safety of their children in school settings, countless claims-makers emerged to assure us that they understood the problem and how best to solve it. The NRA claimed that armed guards should be present in every school, while others wanted teachers and school staff to carry weaponry. One Ohio school district even voted unanimously to allow custodians to "pack heat" after they completed a two-day training course in handgun use. At the time, the local superintendent defended the plan for gun-toting janitors by proclaiming that "sitting back and doing nothing and hoping it doesn't happen to you is just not good policy anymore . . . Having guns in the hands of the right people are not a hindrance. They are a means to protect" (Cavaliere 2013). In Mississippi, Republican representative Philip Gunn urged gun manufacturers "under attack in anti-Second Amendment states" to relocate to his state, where they "will not be criticized for providing goods to law-abiding citizens who enjoy hunting, shooting or who just want the peace of mind that comes with the constitutional right to protect their families" (Martinez and Alsup 2013).

Democratic Representative Carolyn McCarthy (NY) may have taken exception to Gunn's assertion that guns are delivered to law-abiding citizens. She became a leading voice for gun control after her husband was killed and son injured at the hands of Colin Ferguson during the 1993 Long Island Railroad shooting spree in which 5 died and another 19 were wounded. Not long after Sandy Hook, McCarthy introduced legislation to prohibit high-capacity ammunition magazines and called for more stringent regulations on assault weapon availability. Despite considerable public support, McCarthy's hope would ultimately go unrequited. Not only was her bid to eliminate magazine clips that hold more than ten bullets met with resistance, but Senate Democrats also dropped an assault weapons ban from the proposed gun control bill, forcing both measures to be voted on individually, which meant that they could more easily be defeated (Miller 2013). In response to the defeat, McCarthy suggested that gun control legislation routinely fails because of the social authority of the NRA.

> People are afraid to speak out. They're afraid of the NRA. They're afraid of the large lobbyists. And [it's] the same thing with the members of Congress, whether they're Republican or Democrat (Frumin 2012).

CNN further notes that "fierce opposition by the powerful National Rifle Association led a backlash by conservative Republicans and a few Democrats from pro-gun states that doomed key proposals in the gun package, even after they had been watered down to try to satisfy opponents" (Barrett and Cohen 2013). As both of these passages suggest, the NRA's success is underpinned by bold displays of political clout that are crystallized when at-risk politicians in swing states are "reminded" that their constituents are ready to vote them out of office if they fail to tow the line on firearm-related policy matters. In practice, this means that politicians from states like Massachusetts and Vermont can safely contest mandates supported by the NRA because they know there will be little or no political backlash directed at them; legislators that hail from states with strong opposition to firearm restrictions, however, are more likely to acquiesce to the demands of the NRA regardless of whether they personally support or oppose gun control.

Successfully influencing the policymaking process therefore entails more than simply dishing out millions in political contributions and lobbying for a pro-gun agenda. For the NRA it also requires mobilizing opposition to lawmakers that contest unfettered gun rights. Compelling both members and bystander publics to take action can be accomplished in a variety of ways, including direct mailing, telephone solicitation, and online communication. If you peruse the NRA website, you will quickly notice a dynamic multimedia presentation that inundates viewers with claims about the group, its goals, and the urgent need to take action in support of the NRA's heroic work in defending the Second Amendment against politicians that "don't agree with the freedoms that [NRA members] cherish" (Mungin 2013). Take, for example, a video posted on YouTube by the NRA in January of 2013, in which President Obama was accused of being an "elitist hypocrite" for contesting the placement of armed guards at schools across America when his own daughters receive Secret Service protection. Although these types of hyperbolic, morality-laden claims may not be received positively by everyone who views them online, they allow the NRA to reinforce among constituents the message that political opponents do not care about protecting the welfare and Constitutional rights of their loved ones.

Because impassioned moral pleas draw on values that are likely to resonate culturally (Berns 2009), political activists can strategically infuse fervent rhetoric with the explicit hope of producing a strong emotional response. In this sense, associating claims with polarizing public figures serves as a mobilization tool for the NRA to encourage participation in clout building campaigns designed to pressure policymakers into supporting gun rights. This task is further accomplished by grading members of Congress on a scale from A to F based on voting records, public statements, and their responses to an NRA questionnaire, and then publishing those scores on the NRA's Political Victory Fund website. The NRA uses these evaluations to endorse public officials that consistently support NRA-backed mandates and "penalize lawmakers who vote for what it deems 'anti-gun' measures by giving them poor grades in their rating system" (Hunt 2013).

Publicizing how well legislators align themselves with the issue of gun rights reflects how the NRA employs cyber-arenas as platforms to flex its political muscle: Legislators are warned that defying the NRA will have tangible consequences, while NRA-backers can easily identify whether or not specific representatives defend their interests. This latter point is particularly important because claims that resonate as relevant to supporters' own life experiences are more likely to compel a mobilized response. Interested parties, therefore, are not simply told that certain lawmakers are bad; they are confronted with embellished rhetoric couched in notions of patriotism, which clearly delineates the "elitist hypocrites" that oppose gun rights from those who proudly stand with the NRA in "the freedom fight of our lives" (see http://home.nra.org/). Nationalist sentiments underpin many of the claims presented by the NRA and transmit the idea that real Americans do not sit idly by while out-of-touch politicians strip away their liberties. Instead, they fight side-by-side with the NRA in a continuing battle that is being chronicled on the NRA's main site and affiliate webpages through news updates about ongoing campaigns and highlights of past victories. Emphasizing successes in this way allows the NRA to credit loyal public officials for their assistance while also offering demonstrable evidence that each triumph results directly from the contributions of dedicated members.

It is no coincidence that well-financed pressure groups like the NRA maintain professionally designed web pages with catchy visuals, lots of multimedia, and plenty of reminders of how you can get more involved—from joining the NRA, to donating money, or even participating in one of the many gun shows, conferences, and rallies advertised on the site. Users can also customize their experience through a variety of interactive features like "video channels" that offer a variety of ongoing series tailored for specific audiences, which require viewers to return each week to see the latest episode. For example, *NRA News* provides all the latest weekly updates; *NRA Women's* chronicles guns and their owners from a more feminine perspective; and *Life and Duty* presents "Patriot Profiles" of hard-working law enforcement and military personnel who make the world a safer place. Although it may seem like broadcasting a few videos is rather insignificant to pressure groups like the NRA that already have the resources and political might to influence the policymaking process, these tales of personal gun owners and valiant peace officers serve to humanize the NRA and personalize the issue of gun rights by framing an otherwise impersonal lobbying firm as genuinely caring about the needs and values of everyday Americans.

The constant production of new cyber-content combined with emotionally gripping claims about all of the reasons that now is the time for *you* to become involved in the fight for gun rights underscores the important role played by each individual member in the larger success of the NRA: "We're the only firewall standing between your firearm freedoms and those who would take them away, *but we couldn't do it without you* (emphasis added)" (see http://home.nra.org/membership). Presenting materials in this way is presumably intended to foster a sense of intimacy and engagement, as if the NRA is speaking directly to each viewer with impassioned concern about their welfare. This veneer of personal connectedness is continually reinforced through the reproduction of claims that coerce members and casual observers alike to get more actively involved with the NRA (see McAdam 2003). But getting backers into the fold is only half of the battle. Once people identify themselves with groups like the NRA, they still must be aggressively engaged through continued ideological reinforcement. This may include repeatedly explicating the value of the NRA to their way of life, discrediting opponents that attempt to weaken the bond between the NRA and its adherents (McAdam and Paulsen 1993), or focusing on four core elements of e-mobilization: fundraising, voter registration, cyber-activism, and grassroots involvement. The first component deals with financial resource acquisition, such as membership fees and merchandising. The remaining three are intended to rally people toward actions that help the NRA build clout and accomplish its political goals (see McCarthy and Zald 1977).

In conjunction with the Institute for Legislative Action (ILA), which is the lobbying division of the NRA, members are encouraged to use grassroots responses, such as writing letters to lawmakers, attending public events, and participating as an NRA volunteer. The NRA also makes available online petitions and e-mail campaigns that allow people to send a message about protecting gun rights—often prewritten by the NRA—to congressional representatives and media organizations. Similarly, the NRA's "Trigger the Vote" drive is designed to persuade gun owners to complete their voter register so that their voices will be heard during election season. For those lacking the time or interest to make a grassroots contribution, online activism helps maintain involvement in advancing the mission of the NRA at the expense of minimal surplus compassion (Hilgartner and Bosk 1988).[3] This fact is particularly important because we know that both pressure groups and social movements increase citizen involvement by encouraging a sense of solidarity that strengthens members' beliefs that they "share a common fate by virtue of their group affiliation, and that the fate of the individual cannot be separated from the fate of the group" (Rochon 1998, 97). Motivation, then, is inexorably tied to one's sense of personal and collective identification with an issue or faction, and is an important predictor of an individual's willingness to actively participate for a cause (Klandermans and Oegema 1987; Wright and Boudet 2012). To the extent that Internet technology can help advance a group's core mission by lowering the cost of participation, but not necessarily reducing the sense of commitment and achievement, e-mobilization may encourage a greater number of people to more consistently partake in political activism.

DOES LESS REALLY MEAN MORE?

The question that needs to be answered is whether these immediate benefits will translate into long-term success. Larger, more established groups with stable bases like the NRA will inevitably receive greater web traffic than fledging activists, theoretically making it easier to increase membership, conduct fundraising, and build clout with policymakers in online environments. Less reputable claimants might find it much more difficult to realize the true benefits of e-mobilization because potential contributors may simply remain unaware of their existence. Whereas news coverage presents activists' claims to audiences regardless of whether they desire to know that information, online users must actively search for content and may not be inclined to seek out claimants that they do not know exist unless they are directed to do so or happen to accidentally stumble across their websites. We may further question whether the level of dedication generated online is as consequential as that garnered through grassroots efforts. Cyber-activism may only cultivate superficial commitments from participants who need only sit at their computers and send an e-mail or donate some money to feel like they are doing something to advance their chosen cause. Yet these sorts of efforts only confirm that people are willing partake in the shallowest forms of mobilized action, which require little or no industry on their part. As previously noted, the NRA vigorously promotes voter registration to gun owners in cyberspace, provides a rating system on its websites whereby members can target politicians that should be thrown out of office, and publishes online endorsements of preferred lawmakers. Add to this that the NRA spent nearly $11 million on electoral campaigns in 2012, including more than $7.4 million in unsuccessful opposition to President Obama's reelection (UPI 2012). Yet these efforts may have done little to motivate NRA members who had become "complacent because Obama did little on gun control during his first term" (Ingram 2012).

It may very well be that most supporters of the NRA have nuanced political beliefs and consider a variety of factors beyond gun rights when voting for political candidates. Still, greater than 80 percent of NRA-backed candidates won their House or Senate races in 2012, with more than 260 candidates receiving campaign donations totaling approximately $650,000 ($583,646 to Republicans; $74,000 to Democrats). Furthermore, approximately 60 percent of congressional members have received more than $4.3 million in total NRA contributions since 1990; the top recipients of those funds have the highest overall grades and the longest average tenure in Congress (Washington Post 2013). The apparent correlation between NRA approval ratings and the number of years that politicians serve in office might somehow be affected by online clout-building campaigns and voting drives; or, perhaps, the money funneled to those candidates simply allows them to outspend their opponents and manipulate voters with partisan campaign ads. At the very least, if the NRA's true strength derives from its insider status and its ability to fund candidates, then we must consider whether e-mail campaigns and online petitions would really built clout if the NRA did not have access to political backrooms and the financial wherewithal to buy governmental compliance.

There are, of course, examples of people and groups with little social power using the Internet to mobilize people in support of a cause. In 2012, thirteen-year-old McKenna Pope started a petition on the cyber-activism website Change.org to urge the toy maker Hasbro to manufacture its Easy-Bake Oven in gender-neutral colors that would also appeal to boys. More than 44,000 signatures later, Pope and her family delivered the signatures to Hasbro's corporate headquarters, and the company responded by introducing new colors like black and silver to the product line (Grinberg 2012). It no doubt speaks to the dynamism of Internet technology when a young girl can initiate an otherwise innocuous appeal that garners so much public attention it compels a corporate reaction. It certainly helped that the press picked up on the compelling human-interest story of a girl taking on a large corporation and made the public aware of her fight, which surely led additional people to add their names to the petition. Of course, Hasbro had practical reasons for recognizing Pope and offering a supportive response: It provided an opportunity for good public relations, and expanding the available choices on a popular product would presumably be a catalyst for additional sales.

CONCLUSION

There is an undeniable difference between McKenna Pope, whose feel-good story masks the fact that millions of online petitions go virtually unnoticed every day, and the NRA, which has a base of 4 million members ready to visit its website, donate money, and regularly participate in cyber-activism regardless of whether journalists direct public attention to those efforts. Pope succeeded in her Easy-Bake Oven quest with 40,000 signatures and a burst of news coverage that prompted a response from Hasbro. Similarly, in the first 15 hours following Adam Lanza's murder spree at Sandy Hook elementary school, 100,000 digital signatures were added to a White House petition calling for stricter gun control laws.[4] All of that seems quite impressive until we consider that there are over 330 million people in the United States, and petitions supporting the secession of Texas from the Union, the deportation of CNN host Piers Morgan, and the need to stop Google from eliminating its Reader service also garnered more than 100,000 signatures.

None of this is meant to dismiss the importance of cyber-arenas as mobilizing structures, but rather to point out that the lax nature of passive online protest tactics allows the frivolous to intersect with legitimate issues of public concern. In all probability, nobody is going to organize a social movement to prevent the extinction of Google Reader, yet inconsequential online petitions exist side-by-side, and sometimes obtain a bigger response than matters like gun control, human rights, and other public policy matters. Regardless of whether or not this delegitimizes the seriousness of online activism, it might indicate that political claims-makers with less social power will have a more difficult time prompting a resolute mobilized response should online protest come to be viewed as a pointless and flippant exercise dedicated to insignificant issues that do not merit a serious response from policymakers. Part of the problem for claimants is that e-mobilization requires less intensity and commitment than physical protest. It also is not designed to attract news interest or widespread public attention to claimants' efforts.

For the NRA, none of these drawbacks represent an immediate threat to resource acquisition and the mobilization process. Whereas social movements are reliant on media coverage, insiders have perpetual entrée to policymakers. Cyber-arenas, therefore, do not bring needed attention to the NRA so much as marshal needed material (e.g., money) and nonmaterial (e.g., members participating in online activities) resources from its stable advocacy base. For this reason, pressure groups and lobbyists appear to be best positioned to benefit from Internet technology. At the very least, online activism has added legitimacy when performed in conjunction with insider status. Outsiders may find it more difficult to consistently raise public awareness, validate their experience, and achieve favorable political outcomes if they fail to mobilize real-world grassroots responses that redirect media attention toward their claims.. After all, there are countless opportunities for activism available online at any given moment, and we as a society do a pretty good job ignoring most of them.

NOTES

1. These figures fail to include shooting events that are mass in nature or intent but result in fewer than four fatalities. For example, Mark Follman (2013) notes that between the years 2000 and 2010 there were 84 "active shooter" events where the offender's apparent motive was mass murder.

2. The years 2009–2013 are the first time in the history of Gallup polling that Americans have favored protecting economic interests over the environment (Newport 2009; Jones 2010; Saad 2013).

3. Hilgartner and Bosk (1988) define surplus compassion as the amount of time and energy people can devote to causes beyond their immediate, everyday concerns.

4. The petition totaled more than 197,000 signatures on May 1, 2013. A list of all current White House petitions can be found at https://petitions.whitehouse.gov.

Chapter Seven

All the News That's Fit to Post

Big Media and the Shift to Online Coverage

In his seminal book, *The Culture of Fear*, Barry Glassner (1999) writes that the general public is "bamboozled about serious concerns" (3) all the time by public officials, activists, social institutions, and the news media, each of whom profit to some degree by selling us fear. Of the press, he writes that "we have so many fears, many of them off-base, the argument goes, because the media bombard us with sensationalistic stories designed to increase ratings" (xx). Glassner was not specifically writing about online news production, but he might as well have been given the presence of Big Media in cyberspace. Just about every local and national news outlet now maintains a website that is actively updated with the freshest headline stories, and people are turning to the Internet with increasing frequency to learn about the most important news of the day.

At any given time, the decisions made by journalists about what to report online are guided by a prevailing media logic that also influences offline reporting. That is, news tends to be framed as public drama; evocative storylines that draw on broad cultural themes produce "an engrossing story that offers an enticing mixture of compelling characters, dynamic plot, captivating settings, and other story elements" (Monahan 2010, 4). Although journalistic instinct may lead reporters to judge certain things as more newsworthy than others, the logistic and bureaucratic pressures of news work, which require reporters to develop dramatic accounts under the constant pressure of meeting strict deadlines, tends to yield a structured, predictable, and economically feasible standardized news product (Bennett 2005; Fishman 1980; Graber 1988; Shoemaker and Reese 1996; Shudson 1996; Tuchman 1973). Given the practical realities of journalism, it is important to recognize that the choices made on how to report political issues do not simply materialize out of thin air. They reflect choices made by news workers to present social issues according to controversial, dramatic plots that omit "the more complex aspects of [an] issue . . . in favor of a less complicated narrative" (Monahan 2010, 8).

MEDIA CULTURE IN AN ONLINE WORLD

In a March 4, 2013, segment on coal production in the United States, Megan Kelly of Fox News noted that "the whole crackdown on climate change and all that is controversial . . . not everyone believes this is a real issue," and warned viewers that President Obama is trying to destroy the coal industry by waging "an aggressive agenda on the climate with big implication for the country" (Fox News 2013). In addition to funneling precious financial resources to unreliable forms of energy that cost more money to produce, Kelly surmised, the federal government's attempt to promote green energy projects has been a failure: "Even though the President really likes wind and solar and greener energy, the consumers in large numbers do not" (Fox News 2013). The authoritative nature with which the "objective" truth about global warming and the public's disdain of green energy was conveyed to audiences belied that there is no basis in fact for much of what Kelly stated during the report. In fact, there is overwhelming consensus in the scientific community that humans are the primary cause of climate change (Rice 2010), and greater than 70 percent of Americans support increased production of domestic energy using wind and solar power (Jacobe 2013).

Meanwhile, NBC News published on its website a story asserting that two-thirds of all Americans believe global warming is the cause of extreme weather patterns in recent years (Chow 2013), while also reporting the findings from a research study indicating that humans have been contributing to climate change since the nineteenth century (Roach 2013). You might ask how two different news agencies can report such divergent "facts" about global warming when the preponderance of scientific data conclude that man-made climate change is an irrefutable reality. To answer this question, we must go beyond simply assessing the merits of environmental research and understand the reporting logic of mainstream media organizations as it is applied to news stories published online, in print, and across broadcast airwaves. Back when primary news consumption shifted from periodicals to radio and then television, there was a corresponding transformation in how audiences received information because the emphasis moved from the written word to visual imagery. As television evolved and network affiliates began airing local newscasts, reporting soon became less about summarizing important stories and increasingly focused on the sensational nature of breaking news that highlights "mythic confrontations between good and evil, right and wrong, and weak and powerful" (Altheide 1995, 93).

With the advent of television, live, late-breaking reports became the standard, placing viewers on the scene and exposing them to political issues, social actions, and personal behaviors that were once left unseen but now can be observed and scrutinized by millions of people (Doyle 2003; Meyrowitz 1985, 1994). The development of cable news networks that broadcast continuously further changed how stories are reported by fostering a 24-hour news cycle in which investigative information gathering has become secondary to presenting evocative issues that produce a sensory response in viewers (Altheide 2002; Katz 1992). According to Altheide and Snow (1979) an emphasis on entertainment is central to this process; journalists attempt to attract and maintain audiences by providing brief, unambiguous narratives that contain plenty of visual action, dramatic conflict, and emotion (Altheide 1995, 2002; Snow 1983). The advent of Internet technology has only exacerbated this prevailing *media logic*, which favors sensationalism over substance and molds our social reality, regardless of whether or not the information presented to us lacks intellectual depth or factual accuracy (Altheide 2002).[1] Although the most tangible effect of this modern media culture is a declining standard of news quality, there are practical economic reasons that help explain the growing prevalence of *infotainment* journalism in the mainstream press. Advances in communication technology inevitably create greater competition for audience attention by spawning an ever-expanding array of news and leisure options. The growth of cable and satellite television helped foster around-the-clock all-news channels and advertisement-driven programming, both of which have played a role in fragmenting viewers across hundred of available channels and "into many small, relatively exclusive communities of interest that never encounter dissident voices or different points of view" (Webster 2005, 366). In particular, the emergence of networks devoted to niche interests (e.g., ESPN, Home and Garden Television, Style, Animal Planet, and so forth), means that people can learn about the issues of interest to them without ever needing to watch traditional news broadcasts or read any print media.

The Internet and the World Wide Web have further splintered audiences across yet another communication platform that provides countless access points for incredibly fast information retrieval. Whereas there was a time when people learned about the day's events by reading the morning paper, listening to the radio for hourly updates, or watching the evening news, we are now able to search the Internet at our leisure for insight that was traditionally received from the press but now might be made available at a moment's notice to anyone with an Internet connection. Because large quantities of data can be transferred so rapidly online, the press has faced increasing pressure to report stories at breakneck speeds. Consequently, fast-paced mainstream media websites are not designed to necessarily offer audiences depth and contextual analysis, but rather are oriented toward the organizational needs of contemporary news production, which is intended to "organize complex events into familiar, easy-to-grasp communication packages" (Bennett 2005, 44).

All of this places additional constraints on news workers by coercing media organizations to structure reporting practices so that they are increasingly cost-effective to produce, can be easily presented in myriad news formats (from print, to television, and online), and relay narratives that capture audience attention. Reporters hoping not to be out-scooped by fellow journalists or Internet websites are constantly forced to work under the pressure of even tighter deadlines, which often leaves them unable to thoroughly fact-check stories before reporting them to the public. We saw this firsthand in the days after the 2013 Boston Marathon bombing, when John King of CNN proclaimed on air and posted on Twitter that federal authorities had identified a "dark-skinned" male suspect. CNN quickly published a report on its website confirming King's revelation:

> Authorities may have had a breakthrough in the investigation of Monday's Boston Marathon bombings. Investigators believe they have identified a suspect in the Boston Marathon bombings, a source who has been briefed on the investigation told CNN's John King exclusively. The breakthrough came from analysis of video from a department store near the site of the second explosion. Video from a Boston television station also contributed to the progress, said the source, who declined to be more specific but called it a significant development (CNN 2013).

The problem, of course, is that King's "scoop" was wrong and only served to inflame racial tensions despite the fact that federal authorities quickly responded by denouncing the report and claiming on record that no arrest had been made (Wemple 2013). The actual suspects, Dzohokar and Tamerlan Tsarnaev would not be formally identified until the next day, more than 24 hours after CNN personalities had repeatedly reminded viewers that they were using an "abundance of caution" and would not report on any factual matters pertaining to the investigation until they were unequivocally proven to be true (Ladurantaye 2013).

OFFICIAL SOURCES AND THE MANIPULATION OF NEWS COVERAGE

The need to rush breaking news stories to the public combined with the fact that reporters may not have a great deal of scientific or empirical proficiency about the issues they cover results in a greater reliance on current and former public officials, government workers, and corporate professionals to offer credible insight in their specific areas of expertise.

> Journalists will seek to interview them, ask their opinion, and thus introduce them as major news actors or speakers in news reports. If such elites are able to control these patterns of media access, they are by definition more powerful than the media. On the other hand, those media that are able to control access to elite discourse, in such a way that elites become dependent on them in order to exercise their own power, may in turn play their own role in the power structure. In other words, major news media may themselves be institutions of elite power and dominance, with respect not only to the public at large, but also to other elite institutions (van Dijk 1996, 12).

The key here is that a symbiotic relationship exists between news agencies and influential social figures, whereby the press receives the information needed to meet deadlines and break stories in exchange for identifying, citing, and giving credibility to those informants whose claims help shape social reality for audiences (Best 1995; Ericson, Baranek, and Chan 1989; Fishman 1980; Fishman and Cavender 1998).

These *official* sources employ a variety of strategies to get their message out, including scheduled press conferences, daily briefings, designating spokespersons to communicate claims, and sometimes even joining the press as expert correspondents. It is understandable why institutional actors are so valuable to the press: They provide formal statements that are easy to acquire, credible to report, and can be neatly inserted into a standard news story. The police commissioner that gives a press conference about crime control; the district attorney who trots out a victim's family in a high-profile murder case and publically pronounces that she will pursue the death penalty so that the offender feels the wrath of justice; and lawmakers that repeatedly tell you the only thing wrong with this country is their political opponents, are all examples of official sources who can impress their worldview upon us because they have ready access to mass media exposure.

Sociologist Mark Fishman (1980) notes that there are consequences to news coverage that assails audiences with "agency accounts" of social life that "pass on to the public bureaucratic views of the world as plain fact" (136). Namely, politicians and corporate leaders who have the authority to relay their perspectives to you via mass media can frame their ideas as being in everyone's best interest even though they may actually be circulating gross mischaracterizations in order to advance their own political or economic agendas. For instance, public officials routinely disseminate authoritative public statements about out-of-control crime problems that can only be combated with "tough-on-crime" approaches to law enforcement that require "waging war" on some illicit scourge like drugs or terrorism. They do this not because there are empirical data that suggest hyper-punitive social control responses make society safer, but rather because bold responses to combat crime inevitably attract the attention of news agencies, resonate positively with citizens, and help them win reelection. The success of Arizona lawman Joe Arpaio reflects this point. "Sheriff Joe" has become widely recognized as "America's Toughest Sheriff" for adopting a wide array of controversial penal policies that have garnered considerable media coverage over the years. In that time, Arpaio has emerged as a celebrity of sorts who is routinely invited into news cycles as a crime control "expert," which provides a platform for reinforcing his expertise and publicizing his unique brand of social control.

With public approval ratings that often hover near 80 percent (Arpaio and Sherman 2008), Arpaio has become one of most popular elected officials in Arizona (Associated Press 2010; Public Policy Polling 2011). Yet it is the strategic use of mass media that has allowed Arpaio to construct his image as a crime fighter nonpareil with such authority that political elites frequently cite his efforts and seek his input, as reflected in the fact that Republican presidential candidates coveted his endorsement during the 2012 election season (a prize that was ultimately captured by Texas Governor Rick Perry). It is clear to see how news coverage has played an important role in fortifying Arpaio's credibility; but you may wonder how the press really benefits from reporting on a controversial local sheriff who has been investigated by the federal government, had several of his punishment tactics deemed unconstitutional, and offers no empirical evidence that this policies have reduced recidivism (Griffin 2001; Hepburn and Griffin 1998). The simple truth is that Arpaio is a charismatic authority figure whose newsworthiness primarily results from his exaggerated rhetoric, which seems outrageous but falls in line with institutionalized cultural ideologies favoring tough-on-crime approaches (Maratea and Monahan 2013). Consequently, his standing as a law enforcement agent validates his credibility as an expert, while his maverick approach to punishment and justice make him perfectly suited to espouse the discourses of fear and social control that are so prevalent in today's media (Altheide 2002; Simon 2007).

NEWS PRESENTATION ON MAINSTREAM MEDIA WEBSITES

In the end, everyone benefits from the structure of modern news work: public officials like Arpaio get a platform to advance their political agendas; citizens get desired solutions to complex social problems; and news workers get credible reports that may be short on factual accuracy but have a great deal of audience appeal. Considering the logistics that influence the organizational structure of contemporary journalism, it is important to recognize that the news we obtain online from mainstream media websites is guided by the same principles that determine conventional print, television, and radio news production. For this reason, the content published by the press in cyberspace is not entirely dissimilar to what you might find in the morning paper or a nightly newscast. On any given day, headline and breaking lead stories are prominently featured alongside a multitude of links to written reports and video footage of other top news that can range from serious political matters to an in-depth analysis of Miley Cyrus "twerking" on stage. Most likely you'll also find plenty of emotionally gripping tales of crime and disorder with corresponding imagery that helps you visualize the sensational brutality of modern life. Whether it is the account of an Alabama man accused of murdering his cousin for not returning his DVD copy of *The Fast and the Furious* (Associated Press 2013), the horrific saga of Ariel Castro imprisoning three women for more than 10-years, or even the story of a five-year-old child given a fluorescent colored gun designed for kids and then using it to accidentally kill his little sister, the basic premise is the same: The continuous broadcasting of sensational news stories that emphasize drama, conflict, and fear (Altheide 2002; Katz 1992).

Indeed, a defining characteristic of mainstream media websites is a relative standardization of content and structural design. Although no two sites are identical per se, their layouts tend to be remarkably similar: Homepages flooded with top news, multimedia galleries, and sections where users can retrieve popular or heavily viewed articles, weather forecasts, stock market data, sports scores, blogs; and you can even download the news to personal digital devices and access content remotely via podcast or RSS feeds.[2] To make the glut of information presented on these sites somewhat less overwhelming, available news stories are usually categorized according to genre and thus made accessible by going to specifically marked sections like politics, business, opinion, entertainment, and even time-specific topics like the 2012 Presidential election. Spend enough time on these sites and you will soon notice that the news is not much different from what you find on television or in print; there is just more of it available for you to peruse at your convenience.

The sheer abundance of information to be found online means that we have greater access to knowledge that can be obtained with far less effort than at any prior time in human history. Of course, it is sometimes difficult to determine news sources that are genuine in cyberspace from those that simply propagate gossip, lies, and false truths. This may explain why most people tend to access news online from larger, trusted Big Media sources (Pew Research Center 2007a): They know what to expect and may consider mainstream media reporting to be more reliable than alternative sources. Additionally, professional journalism websites offer an extensive variety of content that may appeal to people with diverging interests because the Internet provides an expanded carrying capacity. This simply means that more news can be posted online at any given time than can be comparably present-ed within the strict limitations of print media column space or television airtime (Hilgartner and Bosk 1988). The idea that the Internet expands news availability might seem somewhat counter-intuitive considering that cable news channels broadcast around the clock. But when you watch CNN, MSNBC, or even your local news, you are restricted to learning about only the singular issues being relayed to you *at that moment* by on-air correspon-dents, video footage, and graphical displays, such as on-screen scrolls.

Cyber-arenas, by contrast, can be expanded in a way that allows more reports to be simultaneously reported *and* archived for future availability. Stories that have to be edited out of the standard news hole may be retained online, including older content that may have been previously unavailable or difficult to obtain after its initial publication or broadcast. Add to this the dynamic nature of news presentation on mainstream media websites, which synthesizes the audio and visual elements of print, television, and radio into an easy-to-access package, and Big Media are starting to look more and more alike in cyberspace. Certainly there is no mistaking a copy of *The New York Times* with the television programming on CNN, yet there is a remarkable similarity in structure and presentation found online, which suggests that audiences are being confronted with increased regularization of appearance and content among historically disparate print, television, and radio news organizations.

INTERACTIVITY AND USER CONTROL

The suggestion that all news looks the same is perhaps a bit unsurprising. We know that the evolution of mass media has corresponded with the press developing an increasingly fast-paced, entertainment-oriented approach to news production. Online technology has made today's media environment even more frenetic by escalating the speed with which data flow from their point of origin to recipients, thereby exacerbating the prevailing media cul-ture rather than revolutionizing contemporary journalism. There are novelties to online news consumption, namely the heightened availability of interac-tive tools, such as online polls, reader feedback, and the ability to correspond electronically with members of the press, which have presumably facilitated more active citizen participation in the mass media process (Eveland 2003; Tewksbury 2003). Mainstream news websites also appear to endow people with more authority to search for information that is of specific interest to them: "The hyperlink and menu structure of Web-based news sites provides users with extraordinary levels of control over the news consumption pro-cess . . . it may be that online news selection is guided more purely by readers' interests than is the case with traditional media" (Tewksbury 2003, 696).

This ability to go beyond the relatively narrow scope of press coverage and seek out additional knowledge about issues and events at our own choosing may not be as entirely revolutionary as it seems. Having control over what you look for online makes it easier to acquire "facts" from anonymous or discreditable sources, but it does not necessarily mean that mainstream media are not influencing your search habits. Quite often the hard news (e.g., politics, economics) topics "trending" in cyberspace catch fire only after the public's interest is piqued by news reports that draw attention to those matters.[3] We may question, for instance, whether many people would have paid much attention to the bankruptcy of Solyndra, a company that produced solar cells, were it not for the continued persistence of Fox News and, subsequently, other news outlets in framing the company's failure as an indictment against the viability of green energy, and a possible criminal conspiracy by the Obama administration for guaranteeing millions in federal loans to unsustainable businesses (see Weber 2012). Whatever your personal belief about Solyndra, the point is that the social issues that we think about and search for online are often guided by what the press tell us is important.

As the press continues to influence what we consider to be culturally relevant using online content that is not demonstrably different from what is found in news formats, we are left to wonder whether the enhanced user control offered by online technology amounts to much more than pseudo-citizen participation, which fabricates an illusion of interactivity while news agencies actually make "little effort to take interactive opinions seriously" (Schultz 2000, 209). To this point, there are unmistakable similarities between offline and online versions of traditional news reporting, which remain consistent even when "accounting for value-added items such as links to archived content, audio/visual links, and discussion boards" (Hoffman 2006, 67). Addressing this issue of meaningful involvement is somewhat complex because news outlets provide ample opportunity for audience participation and feedback. Fox News, for example, hosts "UReport," a website where registered "citizen journalists" are given "an assignment description along with some related stories found on FoxNews.com" and then asked to submit photos or video footage related to those topics. CNN's "iReport" similarly allows audience members "to be a part of CNN's coverage of the stories [they] care about" by submitting multimedia or written stories that are published online without any editorial oversight or fact-checking in order to "paint a more complete picture of the news." Likewise, you may have noticed an increasing prevalence of television newscasts devoting a few moments to either read or text scroll across the screen comments submitted by viewers via Twitter and other social media.

While each of these innovations reflects the expansion of audience inter-action with the mass press, they do not necessarily mean that the resulting communication is consequential, or that it plays a role in influencing news agendas. To the contrary, user participation may only serve an ancillary purpose by supplying human-interest tales that generate discussion but lack relevance. It is true that citizen involvement helped break numerous stories in recent years, and there was even a "payola" scandal where a top CNN iRe-porter was found to be purchasing millions of fake hits, or page views, for stories submitted to the site (CNN 2012). Cases like this suggest that mean-ingful exchanges are occurring at some level between journalists and audi-ences. Yet the proliferation of online technology and mobile devices all appear to be most beneficial to Big Media. A 2012 survey by the Pew Research Center found that "the reputation or brand of a news organization, a very traditional idea, is the most important factor in determining where con-sumers go for news, and that is even truer on mobile devices than on laptops or desktops" (Mitchell, Rosentiel, and Christian 2012). Although news now commonly spreads through social media where friends and family can share reports about pertinent issues and events with each other (Pew Research Center 2013b), online consumption nonetheless continues to reflect the fact that most people "have had their basic information needs met by exposure to traditional news media" (Tewksbury 2003, 697).

GATEKEEPING IN A NEW MEDIA WORLD

Regardless of how much authority we have to choose the news stories that we wish to examine in cyberspace, media content ultimately molds our per-spectives of social reality because the press makes us aware of issues and helps shape public opinion (Altheide 2002; Iyengar and Kinder 1987; MacK-uen and Coombs 1981; McCombs 2004; Snow 1983). Journalists invariably assess some claims, issues, and events as being more newsworthy than oth-ers, and the decisions made on what stories to report reflect a *gatekeeping* function that serves to control the flow of information to audiences (Jacobs 2000). This basically means that news workers are continuously determining what is culturally relevant for the rest of society, and the way they frame those matters strongly influences our individual and collective responses. Nowhere is this effect more evident than in the political sphere.

Chances are that you have heard someone toss around accusations of "media bias" whenever an issue is reported in a way that diverges from their preferred ideological disposition. There is little debating that the present media landscape is cluttered with partisan politics and talk shows that appeal to opinion rather than fact, and research indicates that political beliefs influ-ence where people choose to get their news (Prior 2005; Stroud 2010). Communications scholars have described this phenomenon as a process of selective exposure, which essentially means that audiences are drawn to news that strengthens existing predispositions and reinforces what they already believe is true (Klapper 1960). Table 7.1 indicates that the sources of news acquisition varies significantly by political ideology and suggests that specific media outlets have tremendous authority in shaping how people perceive the world around them (Pew Research Center 2011). The 2012 attack on American diplomats in Benghazi, Libya, which left ten people injured and four dead, including U.S. Ambassador J. Christopher Stevens, exemplifies this point. The assault was initially characterized in the press as a spontaneous act. This framing coincided with the official account put forth by the Obama administration; little attention was paid to the possibility that it was a planned terrorist attack, even though many Republicans were espousing that position (Center for Media and Public Affairs 2012).

Persistent coverage by Fox News, whose reporters excoriated President Obama for taking 14 days to declare the strike as an act of terror (Baier 2012), and a string of investigative hearings prompted by Congressional Republicans, would eventually shift the media narrative toward one that questioned why the State Department did not take proper security precautions despite knowing that diplomatic personnel in Benghazi were being threatened by extremists. Nonetheless, Fox News continued to proclaim that the attack had been trivialized thanks to "liberal media spin" bent on protecting the President:

> In the real world, when you cover up four murders after the fact, you likely go to [prison]. In government, you retire with dignity and run for president with full media support . . . The Obama administration has lied, stonewalled, bullied, and intimidated – the true marks of an open and transparent administration. And with few notable exceptions, the American media haven't just let them get away [with] it. Heck, they've helped . . . It wasn't just the traditional media spinning for Team Obama. Lefty outlets did their darndest to downplay the death of four Americans, including the only U.S. ambassador killed since 1979 (Gainor 2013).[4]

By all accounts, Fox News audiences overwhelmingly accepted this version of events. Among those who regularly watch or get news online from Fox News, 55 percent believe that Obama has acted dishonestly, and among Republican audiences that figure rises to a whopping 79 percent.[5] By contrast, only 28 percent of those who do not regularly watch Fox News feel that Obama has been deceitful about the Benghazi incident (Pew Research Center 2013a).

If coverage of the Benghazi incident is any indication, then the mass press continues to influence how people interpret political affairs in the new media age. Still, the proliferation of information availability resulting from Internet

Table 7.1. News source preference by political identity (Pew Research Center 2011)

Source	Total	Solid Liberals	Moderate Dems	Disaffecteds	Libertarians	Moderate Republican	Staunch Conservatives	Bystanders
	%	%	%	%	%	%	%	%
Network News	43	38	47	52	35	51	30	35
Fox News	30	11	31	40	38	37	54	17
CNN	24	27	28	29	15	21	8	16
MSNBC	16	19	20	19	13	18	6	10
NPR	16	24	25	10	17	11	6	6
Daily Newspaper	46	51	34	49	50	55	44	24
The NY Times	6	18	6	3	1	4	1	4
The Daily Show	8	21	3	3	3	3	1	6
Glenn Beck	6	1	6	5	9	6	23	1
Rush Limbaugh	5	2	4	4	9	7	21	1

technology makes it even more difficult to determine the precise impact of mass media on social and political life, which is already muddled by the fact that news imagery is so entrenched in our daily routines (Altheide 1974; DeFleur and Ball-Rokeach 1975). The clichéd power of the press does not simply materialize out of journalists' absolute authority to manipulate your mind and convince you what constitutes the truth. Rather, it is a much more insidious and covert form of control that is tied to the culture industry, which spawns a passive audience of consumers who are repeatedly told each and every day about the how they should respond to the social and political matters that are most pertinent to their lives (see Adorno 1991; Horkheimer and Adorno 1972). Big Media, then, are the cultural lenses through which people learn about and formulate opinions on matters of civic importance.

IS THE INTERNET REVOLUTIONARY OR COMPLEMENTARY?

Despite all the sources of information availability to be found in cyberspace people seem to be funneling back to the proverbial "fourth estate" in online environments. As we have previously discussed, this is partly due to the openness of data flow, which creates trust and reliability problems. Anyone can post just about anything with a veneer of fact; and since we do not necessarily know the specific identities and qualifications of many of the people that choose to publish online, traditional journalism stands as trust-worthy by comparison. That Internet users are funneling to Big Media is indeed a positive development during this time of uncertainty for the news industry. Recent years have seen news agencies suffer from shrinking profit-ability, increased audience segmentation, plummeting print circulation rates, lower television newscast ratings, and a growing reliance on tech companies that provide the software and platforms to transmit news and generate adver-tising revenue in cyberspace. Cutbacks to newsroom personnel have been so severe that almost half of Americans (48 percent) now believe news report-ing is noticeably incomplete in content and analysis, and more than 30 per-cent say that they no longer turn to the press because of declining standards in contemporary journalism (Pew Research Center 2013b).

> In local TV . . . sports, weather and traffic now account on average for 40% of the content produced on the newscasts . . . while story lengths shrink. On CNN, the cable channel that has branded itself around deep reporting, pro-duced story packages were cut nearly in half from 2007 to 2012. Across the three cable channels [CNN, Fox News Channel, and MSNBC], coverage of live events and live reports during the day, which often require a crew and correspondent, fell 30% from 2007 to 2012 while interview segments, which take fewer resources and can be scheduled in advance, were up 31 percent . . . With reporting resources cut to the bone and fewer specialized beats, journal-

ists' level of expertise in any one area and the ability to go deep into a story are compromised (Pew Research Center 2013b).

The outcome in both traditional and online media has been an exacerbation of "infotainment" journalism structured around simplified narratives that contain little or no investigative capacity and are geared more toward sensationalism than substance.

Shifts in communication technology inevitably alter the means by which we acquire information and process knowledge about political life. It is therefore important to recognize that digital technology has not cultivated a fundamental shift away from the entertainment-oriented *media logic* that steers news production (see Altheide and Snow 1979). In addition to the prevalence of shovelware taken from television, print, and radio sources and reproduced on mainstream media websites, reporting is often characterized by catchy headlines, engaging sound bites, and artificial gimmicks, like CNN's "hologram" correspondents (see Welch 2008), at the expense of factual correctness, contextual analysis, and intellectual merit.[6] Perhaps most troubling is that political narratives in contemporary news have become overtly ideological and overwhelmingly negative in their characterization of public officials (Pew Research Center 2011). As journalists have ceded their historic responsibility to simply chronicle civic matters, official sources and other political operatives have been afforded greater authority to manipulate storylines in ways that benefit their bureaucratic and corporate interests. Consequently, news workers acting "as megaphones, rather than as investigators, of the assertions put forward by the candidates and other political partisans" (Pew Research Center 2013b) are unable or unwilling to offer critical assessment, and the reports they produce, which spread so rapidly through cyberspace, simply provide tacit—and sometimes explicit—endorsement of the institutional authority of bureaucratic actors.

CONCLUSION

As new communication technologies emerge, mainstream news agencies must inevitably adapt by developing new strategies for presenting news to the public if they are to maintain their ratings, advertising revenue, and all-important gatekeeping authority. The Internet is merely the latest innovation to challenge the cultural dominance of the press. Time has already shown that the democratizing effects of both print and television have been limited. Professional journalists continue to exert tremendous authority in disseminating information throughout society, and public perceptions continue to reflect messages received from news media sources. This is not to suggest that the Internet does not provide important new forums for interactions that can increase citizen participation in the public sphere: message boards, chat rooms, blogs, and even sites like YouTube are indicative of this fact. Certainly the press has been forced to address the changing nature of information distribution by developing new techniques for rapidly publishing reports that are adaptable to online environments. Social media, podcasts, smart phone apps, and widgets are all platforms by which news can be transferred to audiences in cyberspace and then shared among family, friends, or anyone else we choose.

You may have even noticed that television news, particularly programs airing on around-the-clock cable channels, is starting to mirror some of the elements found on mainstream media websites. Colorful graphics tend to fill the screen along with news tickers that display important headlines, and broadcasts are becoming increasingly interactive. For instance, viewers of the "Ed Show" on MSNBC are asked by host Ed Schultz to text message responses to daily poll questions; and for most of 2010, former CNN anchor Rick Sanchez read on-air audience feedback sent via social networking sites like Twitter during his show "Rick's List." The media convergence does not end there. News organizations are now entering into working partnerships that enhance their ability to get more information to consumers. NBC News and *The New York Times* agreed to share content during the 2008 presidential election, and more recently ABC News and Yahoo formed an alliance that "blends ABC News' global newsgathering operation . . . with Yahoo! News' unmatched audience, depth and breadth of content" (ABC News 2011). Additionally, staffing cutbacks have resulted in more outsourcing of newsgathering to external sources such as nonprofits and research firms that provide information, which can easily be inserted into reports alongside an attribution that identifies the source of the material (Pew Research Center 2013b).

There are drawbacks, of course, to supplementing stories with data extracted from non-journalistic sources: PR firms, activists, and others with political motives will inevitably find ways to insert propaganda into reports unbeknownst to audiences and the editorial staffs that approve them. While this reflects the diminished quality, reliability, and objectivity of political reporting, the press nonetheless seems best positioned to capitalize on the "cyber-news" market. At any given moment there can be millions of claims floating through cyberspace. Clearly it is not possible to learn about all of them; there simply is not enough time in the day. So we need a filtering mechanism to inform us about the most germane matters affecting our lives and the larger social welfare. Given the surplus of information that the Internet has added to our lives, Big Media have perhaps developed an even more important role as cultural gatekeepers. News consumers might be critical of the press, but they also tend to consider professional reporting to be more dependable than the alternatives popping up online. Mainstream media websites, therefore, have become an access point for audiences, helping them make sense of their world by identifying and summarizing the most important stories of the day. As the press continues to adapt and enhance its own online presence – newspapers, for example, might be entirely online in the near future – we may expect to see an increasing array of content availability on corporate news websites in an effort to combat audience fragmentation and ward off competition from independents and citizen journalists. Regardless of how this plays out, Big Media ratings, circulation rates, and profits have all been in precipitous decline. The Internet may hold the best hope for reversing that trend.

NOTES

1. Anthony Downs (1972) argues that issues "must be dramatic and exciting to maintain public interest because news is 'consumed' by much of the American public (and by publics everywhere) largely as a form of entertainment" (42). Contemporary scholarship examines the exacerbation of this reporting "logic" as news agencies compete for audience attention against an ever-expanding array of entertainment and leisure options.

2. Podcasts are audio or video files that can be downloaded to a personal computer or portable device; RSS (Really Simple Syndication) involves users subscribing to a website's feed format, which they then can peruse at any time to check for new or updated content published on that site.

3. Citizen-generated content does sometimes generate significant attention in cyberspace, such as when a home video "goes viral"; but these instances are often related to human interest stories rather than hard news.

4. It is worth noting that Dan Gainor, the author of this particular editorial published on the Fox News website, is a Fellow at the Media Research Center, an ideologically conservative media "watchdog" group. His characterization of news coverage reflects how easily partisan operatives can be presented to audiences as experts with unbiased empirical data that defend their "objective" positions.

5. Among Republicans that do not regularly watch Fox News, the percent of respondents who believe Obama has acted dishonestly lowers to 60 percent (Pew Research Center 2013a).

6. According to a report posted on the technology website C/Net, CNN is actually using faux holograms because the images are produced by placing a correspondent in front of a green screen and then filming them simultaneously with 35-high definition cameras: "If CNN was truly using a "hologram," it would not have employed a green screen and overlay images. Instead, it would have captured scattered light and then reconstructed it back in the studio" (Reisinger 2008).

Chapter Eight

Conclusion: Old Wine in New Bottles?

Changes in information technology invariably influence the ways individuals think about social and political life (Altheide et al. 2001). Cyber-optimists have heralded the Internet as a transformative technology that will produce revolutionary social change by increasing civic participation in the public sphere (DiMaggio et al. 2001; Katz and Rice 2002; Surratt 2001; Williams and Delli Carpini 2000, 2004). This presumed democratization effect is rooted in the belief that online technology can engender greater civic involvement and stems from the fact that large amounts of information flow freely throughout cyberspace without the time and space limitations that are inherent in offline interaction, thereby (1) creating more informed citizens and (2) facilitating the growth of online communities comprised of people who share common interests, experiences, and beliefs, (Beetham 2006; Berman 2003; Wellman et al. 2001). The breadth of available information online combined with the ability to cheaply publish content for widespread audiences void of any governmental or institutional editorial oversight will supposedly produce an engaged global citizenry that demands greater accountability from journalists, public officials, and corporate leaders.

While these expectations might be somewhat ambitious, there is no denying that the Internet has transformed many aspects of public life. The Internet does provide a global forum for sharing ideas and facilitates the development of mediated interpersonal associations, which can potentially foster a sense of empowerment, even among historically disenfranchised populations (Rapp et al. 2010). Romantic, indeed, is the notion that everyone online exists in a state of virtual equality, irrespective of real-world power differentials. Still, this idyllic vision of an information superhighway that enables "ordinary people to have access to knowledge . . . [and] . . . causes a profound shift in power towards its consumers" (Beetham 2006, 238) is not completely without merit. At least in theory, all people with Internet connections do have the potential to be active producers of information, even if they have little or no control over audience interest. This in itself is significant, given that citizen journalists have already shown that given the right circumstances they can influence mainstream news agendas. Likewise, online technology has produced countless new social networks that provide individuals with public forums through which they can obtain information, express their beliefs, communicate with colleagues, debate opponents, and disseminate problem claims to worldwide audiences.

Internet enthusiasts ultimately foresee a world where cyber-technology will "promote open, democratic discourse, allow for multiple perspectives, and mobilize collective action" (Wellman et al. 2001, 438). To a degree this vision has been somewhat realized. The public sphere has undergone a fundamental transformation in the new media age. This is readily apparent anytime you turn on the news and see amateur video footage taken on a cell phone, read a report about how someone has gotten into legal trouble because of something they posted on a social media site, or even when you first discovered that you can be arrested for communicating information online that another person unbeknownst to you deems to be threatening. A seventeen-year-old Michigan teen learned this lesson firsthand after she was fired by her employer for posting an offensive Tweet about the death of Trayvon Martin (Abbey-Lambertz 2013). Likewise, an otherwise innocuous Facebook argument about the online game *League of Legends* led to the arrest of nineteen-year-old Justin Carter:

> Carter was called "crazy" by the person he was arguing with, and according to the arrest warrant, Carter responded by saying, "I'm fucked up in the head alright, I think I'ma shoot up a kindergarten and watch the blood of the innocent rain down and eat the beating heart of one of them." . . . This comment was seen across the Web, and a woman in Canada took a screen shot of the exchange, reporting it to Canadian Crime Stoppers. The photo was turned over to U.S. authorities and . . . Carter was arrested for making terrorist threats (Wilcox 2013).

On a grander scale, the travails of Bradley Manning, Edward Snowden, and a host of other whistleblowers whose use of online technology to expose previously hidden elements of the social order has called into question our understanding of what constitutes freedom of speech in the new media world.

The consequences of these ongoing debates about Internet freedom may not seem to have immediate relevance in our day-to-day lives. Most likely, only our family and friends—along with few hackers, identity thieves, and NSA agents—are particularly interested in the things we do or post online. Yet, our interaction with cyber-arenas nonetheless guarantees that what we communicate via the Internet is global in scope. If you are not seeking an audience, or have not accidentally found one, then the ability to communicate on such a grand scale might not strike you as all that important. But for political activists and other claimants that desire a social voice, the implications are profound: "The Internet is a boon to claims-makers in that Web sites, discussion groups, and blogs can be established quite easily and at minimal cost. Claims of all sorts can be posted and made accessible to anyone who knows how to use a search engine; in effect, the Internet has an unlimited carrying capacity . . . In addition to these considerations . . . improved communications (such as the World Wide Web) give people around the world access to claims made in distant places, and at least some of those claims will be theorized in terms that make it easier for them to spread" (Best 2008, 141, 306).

On one hand, this means that the Internet equips claims-makers with a dynamic public forum to disseminate claims on a mass scale. However, it also suggests that Internet users have ready access to an increasingly wide array of diverse claims pertaining to a broad range of political issues. In other words, the ability to publicize claims and have them disperse through cyberspace does not guarantee that they will connect with prospective supporters, because the Internet has increased audience fragmentation. The sheer volume of information available online combined with the vast number of individual web spaces allow people to customize their Internet experience by either creating their own, or perusing others' arenas dedicated to their particular topics of interests. Whereas audiences tend to passively consume the news presented to them by journalists via traditional media formats like television, print, and radio, they have a greater ability to determine what content they search for online—even if those decisions are often determined by what issues are framed as culturally relevant by the mainstream press—which may ultimately expose the average news consumer to a narrower range of perspectives.

The extent to which cyber-arenas allow individuals to search out issues of specific interest to them while avoiding exposure to counter-claims and alternative viewpoints that challenge their outlook is relevant, but not necessarily all that revolutionary given that audience fragmentation is hardly unique to the Internet. Television broadcasters, for example, routinely market news and entertainment programming "at particular demographic groups . . . because people fitting a particular demographic profile (defined by age, sex, income, and so on) are more likely to watch programs aimed directly at their interests" (Best 2008, 140). The Internet, in turn, has exacerbated the affects of viewer segmentation: Whereas there are hundreds of television channels, content can spread at incredibly fast speeds across millions of online web spaces, many of which extend beyond the purview of media conglomerates that control mainstream media production. To consumers the benefits are greater choice; we have more options than ever before to tailor the things we watch, read, and hear according to our particular niche interests. Political activists and other types of claims-makers, however, are faced with a double-edged sword. Publicizing claims and mobilizing support online to global audiences for relatively little cost are enticing benefits that can potentially extend claimants' public relevance and help fledgling activists remain solvent for longer than would otherwise be possible if they did not have an Internet presence. Consequently, cyber-arenas may help foster the growth of emerging social movements prior to the materialization of a newsworthy crystallizing event that attracts media attention.

Of course, it is conceivable that political activism fostered primarily in cyberspace will eventually attain social traction without the Internet. But we may speculate that online technology can hasten its growth by providing the necessary vehicle for supporters to both identify advocates that share their beliefs and unify around a common purpose. The problem, though, is that online technology may simultaneously hinder the growth, viability, and relevance of political claimants. Because the Internet expands the capacity to carry claims beyond what the press can report to the public while filling the standard news hole, a greater diversity of claims is flooding the marketplace at any given point in time. Although it might seem counterintuitive, having more claims made publically available from a greater array of activists actually increases competition for already scarce public attention needed to validate a political movement or issue, recruit powerful allies, attract the attention of public officials, and, most importantly, obtain precious news coverage. In truth, the vast majority of claimants will never have any measurable effect on the political process. For every instance of a blogger breaking a scandal, citizen journalist capturing compelling video footage, or whistle-blower exposing confidential information online, there are countless others whose contributions go unnoticed amidst the vast expanse of cyberspace. The Internet may indeed provide the lay citizenry as a whole with a greater and more impactful voice in the public sphere. But most individuals (and activists, for that matter) in isolation are unlikely to have cultural significance and exert any influence over social discourse or mainstream news agendas because they attract only meager audiences that largely consist of friends and family. Simply put, most Internet users will go through life without even being aware that many, if not the majority, of publically available web spaces actually exist.

This in itself is troubling given that claims-making is essentially a process wherein activists use rhetorical techniques to deliver claims related to what they perceive to be troubling social conditions in hopes of attracting media attention that delivers their concerns to the largest possible audience. When news coverage redirects public interest toward a particular political issue or event, people sometimes demand that something be done to address the situation, thereby pressuring policymakers to take action, often through legislation or the adoption of governmental standards designed to rectify the problem. As this book has attempted to show, the Internet offers political claimants a dynamic platform for communicating directly with prospective supporters and disseminating unfiltered claims to a global populace. Yet these benefits do not replace, or even substantively undermine, the fundamental need for mainstream news coverage to pique public interest about issues, activists, and claims that they may never have otherwise been exposed to regardless of their availability in cyberspace.

While this suggests that the process by which political activists gain recognition remains remarkably similar to previous eras, the introduction of digital, wireless, and online technologies have nonetheless resulted in several important contributions. First, the Internet appears well suited to accommodate news production that synthesizes well with the entertainment-oriented reporting logic that characterizes contemporary journalism. Claims that lack novelty and dramatic value and fail to resonate with audiences are not likely to gain widespread recognition regardless of whether they are published online or using traditional claims-making tactics. In addition, the Internet has empowered motivated citizens to take a more active role as political claimants and citizen journalists; and some on occasion have proven to successfully alter political and news agendas. Since cyber-arenas have theoretically limitless carrying capacities, claims can be disseminated around the clock and archived in virtual perpetuity for relatively little cost compared to other techniques like direct mailing and telephone solicitation. The Internet has also spawned new communication networks and forms of activism such as e-mail campaigns, virtual marches, and online petitions, each of which allow supporters to be *e-mobilized* into action without ever having to leave their homes.

PLACING THE "NET EFFECT" OF POLITICAL CLAIMS-MAKING IN HISTORICAL CONTEXT

Each of these contributions is important in that they expand upon our understanding of how political claims-making functions in the Internet age. Less clear, however, are the long-term implications of online activism and e-mobilization, which tend to be fundamentally passive and often involve little more than sitting at a computer and sending an e-mail or making a donation. Addressing this issue requires that we try to identify the *marginal effectiveness* of political claims-making and protest practices in cyberspace; that is, do they yield significantly favorable results for a broader faction of citizens and at less cost than more traditional forms of activism and moral entrepreneurship (see Becker 1963)?[1] This book has not necessarily sought to empirically answer the question of marginal effectiveness, but instead to critically assess the whether the Internet is reshaping the processes of claims-making and political protest. Online technology undoubtedly endows people who were once removed from the media process to actively become "citizen journalists," or perhaps more appropriately, "citizen claims-makers."

Perhaps it is unsurprising that cyber-optimists have hailed this achievement as reflecting the transformation toward a more ideal society where everyone can communicate freely within a democratized public sphere given that similar claims have been made about other technological advancements throughout history. We can trace the liberating effects of communication technology to the invention of the printing press in 1440; it made available to a greater number of people—generally the literate members of the middle classes—written materials previously monopolized by social elites within the state and church. Suddenly hundreds of texts could be produced in the same amount of time that it had previously taken to copy a single book by hand. From an historical perspective, the invention of movable type was the initial catalyst for what centuries later would become the mass press. Although broad, sweeping social change was not immediate, and rising literacy rates were initially as reliant on the growing need for greater social and economic innovation among those groups (e.g., the Church, government, private employers) who require a literate workforce as the production of the printing press itself, cheap mass production extended the availability of periodicals to previously excluded segments of the population.

The developments of telegraph and the telephone were similarly hailed as transformative because they allowed for information to be shared swiftly across disparate locations. James Gleick notes that when Charles Morse transmitted his first line of code in 1844, the notion of synchrony, or the occurrence of simultaneous action, was so unimaginable that it had "originated in the mind an entirely new class of ideas, a new species of consciousness. Never before was any one conscious that he knew with certainty what events were at that moment passing in a distant city—40, 100, or 500 miles off . . . It requires no small intellectual effort to realize that this is a fact that *now* is, and not one that *has been*" (*The New York Herald* as quoted in Gleick 2011, 149, emphasis in original). Likewise, radio was praised for offering audiences greater immediacy to experience events as they happened than was ever possible with print media: "Radio meant for the first time in history one person with a microphone could speak to many, influence them, and perhaps change their lives" (Lewis 1992, 26). Proponents argued that radio broadcasting would progress society into a new age of civility (Jewett 1974; Vanobberghen 2010), and because governmental interests had no direct control over what people listened to in their homes, the household radio was hailed as a revolutionary technological breakthrough. Of course, nobody could really listen to anything they wanted; most were forced to hear what operators at major stations or independent amateurs chose to play over the airwaves.

Oftentimes audiences could not hear anything at all as the sheer number of broadcasters fighting for space on the same frequency cancelled out each other's signal.

In order to resolve the glut, the federal government eventually passed the Radio Act of 1927, which established formal permission from the government was needed to use public airwaves (DeFleur 1966; Krattenmaker and Powe 1994). Burgeoning regional and coast-to-coast networks operated by big corporations like the National Broadcast Company (NBC) and the Columbia Broadcast System (CBS) soon overran amateurs that previously had the freedom to broadcast on deregulated airwaves (Davis 1974; Emery, Ault, and Agee 1973). By the early 1940s, the voice of radio was, for better or worse, limited to a select group of elite media conglomerates, marking a major shift from its inception when radio was not unlike the Internet: A deregulated communication medium that allowed both professional and citizen broadcasters equal access to the airwaves.

The shift toward corporatized mass media ultimately left the power of the press in the hands of commercial news agencies (Bagdikian 1997; Kurtz 1998), even though the emergence of the household "picture box" would lead many to believe that television had "the potential to contribute to a more informed, inclusive, and nonpartisan democracy" (Gurevitch, Coleman, and Blumler 2009). Audiences were no longer restricted to merely reading about the political upheaval caused by the fight for civil rights in the newspaper, or listening to news reports about the atrocity of war. They could now view from their own homes nightly news footage of protesters being beaten by police, Alabama Governor George Wallace's stark bigotry while giving his "Stand in the Schoolhouse Door" speech in opposition to the desegregation of the University of Alabama, and the bodies of American soldiers lying dead and wounded on the combat fields of Vietnam. In response a growing number of people began to press policymakers to enact civil rights reform and popular sentiment eventually turned against the Vietnam War.

The force of television became so powerful that it eventually reshaped the social, political, and media landscape, leading advocates to suggest that it too would produce a more equitable and participatory democracy by motivating a previously uninspired citizenry through the greater availability of political information. It is perhaps ironic, then, that two of the top-rated television programs in the early- to mid-1960s were *The Beverly Hillbillies* and *The Andy Griffith Show*, which both portrayed Southerners as congenial, understanding people, and depicted no African Americans living in either a small North Carolina town or a large, urban metropolis like Los Angeles. Notwithstanding that Watts was exploding with race riots and the civil rights movement was gaining a social foothold, network executives presented a whitewashed version of American life on television. This is the fundamental paradox of visual mass media: It can expose audiences to previously hidden elements of social and political life, yet they are restricted to seeing only what broadcasters choose to show them.

The average citizen has historically had little influence on mass media and the day-to-day functioning of political power. What we know about current affairs we generally learn from news reports—or from other people who tell about what they read or saw in the news—filtered through the traditional press. Throughout this book we have examined how different types of political claims-makers use the Internet to achieve the democratic ideals not fully realized through television, radio, and print by attempting to get their message to us directly in online settings and indirectly via news media coverage. Because there is no longer a single axis by which news workers reach the public, we are now bombarded with a frenetic flow of information bursting online thorough a "multiplicity of gates . . . both in terms of sheer numbers and sources" (Williams and Delli Carpini 2004, 1213). Whereas there are now hundreds of television channels—a fraction of which are dedicated to politics all or part of the time— claims can go "viral" and rapidly spread across millions of different web spaces. This combined with the volume of political information available online allows users to customize their own web experience by creating their own cyber-arena, or perusing other sources dedicated to their particular interests—many of which can be defined as alternative media because they are not operated by mainstream news organizations. It also means that claimants themselves have a multitude of new ways to connect with audiences in hopes of mobilizing them into action.

Of the citizen journalists, activists, pundits, and practitioners that have benefited from online technology, the burgeoning paradigm of cyber-activism is passive resistance, and online public discourse tends to be characterized by open partisanship. Although further research on audience effect is needed, it is reasonable to suspect that the Internet filters people toward claims that they support. In other words, cyberspace can be a tool for confirming opinionated views about strongly held beliefs, many of which are initially cultivated, in part, using information obtained from *fair and balanced* traditional news sources. The tendency toward selective exposure really is not all that surprising given that alternative websites offer political information that has not been verified by any institutional editorial oversight, and professional news agencies continue to cover hard news coverage with an increasingly ideological "soft" opinion-based approach that provides an open platform for bureaucratic actors and political figureheads to push their agendas virtually unchallenged. Quite simply, Internet technology has synthesized well into the superficial, partisan, and entertainment-oriented culture of modern political news coverage.

FROM BACK ROOMS TO CHAT ROOMS: PERSISTING SOCIAL POWER DISPARITIES IN CYBERSPACE

While the Internet may indeed empower citizens journalists and fledgling political activists, the dynamics of social power in the new media world remain largely unchanged: Elites continue to influence public opinion while the powerless, for the most part, remain disenfranchised. Influential lobbyists and political insiders still have a distinct competitive advantage in getting their issues recognized by journalists, policymakers, and the public at large. Chances are that if you watch a television newscast or search online for the top stories of the day, you are probably going to see political reports that have been endorsed as relevant by authoritative political and economic figures. Consider the so-called Birther movement, which contends that Barack Obama is not a natural born citizen of the United States and is therefore ineligible to be President. While average citizens have played a role in cultivating the birther conspiracies, the bulk of the media coverage was been reserved for conservative politicians like Michelle Bachmann and Mike Huckabee, who initially failed to openly acknowledge President Obama's natural born citizenship, expressed skepticism of it, or even proposed legislation requiring candidates for public office to provide a certified, long-form version of their birth certificate.

If news coverage of the Birther movement tells us anything, it is that for all of the ways that the Internet has supposedly facilitated a more egalitarian public sphere, our understanding of the issue is still largely predicated by mainstream news reports that are predominately framed by members of the polity. This is not a matter to be considered lightly. Considerably more news time is dedicated to Donald Trump talking about his good relationship "with the Blacks," or making preposterous investigative efforts to find President Obama's long-form birth certificate simply because he is a widely recognizable figure than will ever be granted to you, me, and most of the influential scholars working in academia; and this is not something new that we can attribute to the Internet. Back in 1989, Donald Trump made headlines by calling for the public execution of five New York City teens, four of which were African American and the other Hispanic, after they were charged with brutally raping Trisha Meili when she was jogging through Central Park. The only problem: All five teens were innocent, having been railroaded by authorities into giving false confessions that helped secure their wrongful convictions.

Anecdotally, Trump's cultural and media relevance does little to dispel Howard Becker's (1963) notion that moral entrepreneurs are persons or groups of affluence. Cyber-activism and online claims-making may indeed be easier and cheaper than offline techniques like mass mailings, cold calling, and organizing public protests, but the financial cost and time commitment is likely to be nonetheless prohibitive for most people in a position of economic hardship. In many ways, the idea that the Internet gives voice to anyone is true only in theory. One must first be able to afford the equipment needed to maintain an active web presence, which includes both the monthly fees for a high-speed online connection and the bandwidth or provider costs to operate a website. Participating in the political process in any capacity also requires that a person have sufficient time and surplus compassion above and beyond the concerns of everyday life to participate meaningfully in some form of activism. Political change ultimately entails tremendous effort and sacrifice among those most committed to the cause, and online technology does not change that fact.

Where would we be if Earl Gideon had simply been able to add his name to an online petition instead of submitting a hand written appeal for a writ of certiorari to the Supreme Court challenging the constitutionality of his being denied legal representation? What about if all of the heroic champions for civil rights, people like Dr. Martin Luther King, Jr. and Representative John Lewis, had decided to send an e-mail to their local Southern white congressman rather than risk their own well-being to protest in the streets for equality? Perhaps it is cliché, but there is a price to be paid for social progress; and in this regard, the true Internet effect on political claims-making and contemporary activism might actually be counter-intuitive, serving to reaffirm and expand state, corporate, and media control. The dissemination of cyber-claims and online protest tactics may indeed "get people more involved in public life, facilitate the formation of social networks (social capital), and contribute to participatory and deliberative democracy" (Park and Perry 2008, 192), but those efforts collectively place little pressure on political institutions because they are trivial in scope, often brushed aside as inconsequential by political and corporate leaders, and may increase the hegemonic authority of bureaucratic actors who recognize that the Internet creates a diversion that minimizes the likelihood of a street-level response, while doing very little to pressure the powers that be into enacting social reform.

There is a telling scene in the Michael Moore documentary *Sicko*, when a woman states that in the U.S., Americans are afraid of the government, while in France politicians are afraid of the people. Her point is that the periods of dissatisfaction prompt the French to picket, protest, and strike until the state responds to their demands—all things that Americans are socialized to believe undermine the moral fabric of our society. When the Chicago teachers union authorized a strike in the fall of 2012 to protest unsatisfactory working conditions, the general response from Fox News was to fire all of the "greedy, selfish union teachers" and then simply "bring in substitutes and supervisors from across the state. Offer them full time jobs at one-third lower salaries, one-half the pensions, and demand bigger contributions for their health care costs. And tell them the school day just got 2 hours longer" (Root

2012). The point to be had here has nothing to do with teachers' unions at all; it is about our tendency to sit idly by while the standard of middle-class life deteriorates as the rich get richer while the rest of us flatline, the justice system continues to prey on the powerless, and the government intrudes more and more on our rights in the name of protecting us against terror. Sure, there was the Occupy movement, which was a grassroots, street-level effort at protesting economic inequality. But it was easily discredited as a frivolous collective full of misguided youth with no centralized message that, in the long run, accomplished little more than cause an inconvenience to commuters traveling to and from their places of work.

As Occupy suggests, not all physical protest efforts flourish, but every successful social movement is characterized by fervent grassroots mobilization that activists have thus far been unable to duplicate in cyberspace. In many ways, the Internet has been a pretty good development for those in power who can use the technology to communicate with constitutents, put forth their agendas, and construct populist veneers that generate a favorable response from voters. Perhaps you remember during the 2012 presidential election when it seemed like a new photograph popped up every day showing President Obama drinking a beer with fellow citizens on the campaign trail. More recently the Obama administration drew attention for cheekily responding to a White House petition to begin construction on a *Star Wars*-like Death Star by 2016 (Shawcross 2013). While institutional actors and political insiders might sometimes—and perhaps often—come under scrutiny in the press for their actions, they also have the ability to use the Internet in a way that constructs endearing narratives about themselves that the press are usually all too happy to relay to us when we watch or read the news.

Still, the power of Internet technology for insiders and members of the polity can be far more insidious and actually function to expand the scope of social and bureaucratic control. We have been witness over the last few decades to government authorities utilizing digital technology to vastly expand their dominance over the larger citizenry. In the U.K., political leaders are attempting to require Internet service providers (ISP) to install devices to monitor all online traffic in a move that exponentially expands the government's ability to conduct surveillance in cyberspace (Gayle 2013). Not to be outdone, the Obama administration supports a plan to extend the FBI's ability to wiretap people that communicate online (Savage 2013), despite concerns from technology experts that such measures may inflict serious harm on everyday Internet users (Sengupta 2013). We must also consider the prospect of a more corporatized Internet at some point in the future, which would likely serve to restrict the visibility in cyberspace of average people and outsider activists. Should a two-tiered Internet emerge wherein telecommunications companies allow ISPs that use their networks to charge additional fees for faster delivery of certain content, well-funded corporations, institutions, and political insiders that can afford the added cost of high-speed transmission would be given priority over those with limited resources, whose web spaces would be more difficult to access.

Regardless of whether these sorts of governmental actions ever have a noticeable presence in our lives, they reflect the fact that cyber-utopian notions of a democratized public sphere mask the reality that those people and groups with political and economic power can use online technology as a mechanism to expand social control and disseminate propaganda. Blindly committing ourselves to the belief that the Internet will change everything can therefore preclude us from really seeing all the ways that technology controls us rather than expanding our freedoms (Morozov 2011). Margaret Beetham (2006) has noted that "at this historical moment it is not so much the fact of changing technologies as the pace of change which threatens to dissolve to solidities of the past" (231). Perhaps she is right and the real issue is that rapidly developing advancements in communication media make it more difficult for the polity to control them. Whether or not this is the case, sometime in the future the next great thing will come along and replace the Internet. It, too, will likely transform society and broaden the ways by which people are able to communicate. This new technology will undoubtedly be democratizing to a degree; but if history is any indication, it will also be co-opted by corporate and political actors to expand their influence over larger society.

The German philosopher Herbert Marcuse (1964) once wrote that powerful social elites use technology to control people's lives, all while the individuals being manipulated continue believe that those very technologies have liberated them to live more comfortable lives in advanced industrial societies. This is the ultimate paradox: communication technologies are simultaneously liberating and mechanisms for bureaucratic social control. In cyberspace we can anonymously participate in the free-flow exchange of ideas, yet we are more visible than ever before to government surveillance, corporate marketing, and scam artists that lurk in the shadows of the information superhighway. Amateur claimants have a greater social presence than ever before, even as their voices are routinely drowned out by the institutional actors that continue to determine what political and social issues are most relevant to our lives, while manipulating our thoughts on how best to respond to them. Your own personal view of technology might not be as dystopian as Marcuse, but nor should you simply assume that the Internet has revolutionized political activism by truly democratizing the public sphere. At the very least, it would seem that the medium has not really changed the message all that much.

NOTES

1. Howard Becker (1963) defines moral entrepreneurs as affluent individuals or groups with the initiative to create and enforce social rules.

Methodology Appendix

The primary methodological approach used for this book is qualitative document analysis (QDA), which allows the researcher to identify recurring themes and patterns and their relevance in documents in order to better "understand the communication of meaning, as well as to verify theoretical relationships" (Altheide 1987, 68). Since, QDA is fundamentally reflexive in nature, "categories and variables initially guide the study, but others are allowed and expected to emerge throughout the study, including an orientation toward *constant discovery* and *constant comparison* of relevant situations, settings, styles, images, meanings, and nuances (emphasis in original)" (Altheide 1996, 16). This is generally accomplished through the collection of numerical (e.g., counts) and narrative (e.g., frames, themes) data, with the goal of expanding, replacing, or even refuting existing theoretical statements (Altheide 1996). For QDA to be an appropriate methodological choice, all acquired data—both in terms of print and multimedia reports, and web pages—were approached as documents that could be analyzed for both manifest and interpretive content (see Berg 2006, 242). As Altheide (1996) notes, a document is a "symbolic representation that can be recorded or retrieved for analysis" in order to "understand culture—or the process and the array of objects, symbols, and meanings that make up social reality shared by members of a society" (2). Just as newspapers, television newscasts, and radio broadcasts can be defined as primary documents used to analyze the dissemination of claims, so too can a web page be viewed as an electronic document; the format is novel, but the content therein (e.g., print, audio, video) is not necessarily distinct from other types of documents.

In order to gain a better understanding of how these online documents are used by claims-makers, instrumental case studies were utilized to show the processes by which political claims, networking structures, and mobilization efforts are fashioned in cyberspace. The value of using instrumental case studies is that they help provide insight into a given issue or refine a theoretical account: "In these situations, the case actually becomes of secondary importance. It will serve only a supportive role, a background against which the actual research interests will play out . . . the intention is to assist the researcher to better understand some external theoretical question or problem" (Berg 2006, 229). For this particular monograph, case studies provide a means for applying social constructionist theories to explain cyber-activism and media reporting of political claims in cyberspace. Each case study was conducted using a standardized QDA approach that involves five key stages: (1) identify documents, (2) data collection and protocol design, (3) data coding, (4) data analysis, and (5) integration of findings into a final report (Altheide 1996, 23). Although QDA provides the researcher with the flexibility to subjectively interpret data (Altheide 1996), attempting to maintain uniformity in method of analysis is nonetheless important to ensure analytical consistency.[1] The following sections detail additional methodological procedures that are specific to particular chapters in the book:

CHAPTER 3: POWER TO THE PEOPLE? CITIZEN JOURNALISM IN CYBERSPACE

QDA was used in this chapter to analyze how "Rathergate" was a blog-driven controversy that succeeded in attaining mass media attention. Data for this chapter were acquired in two distinct phases. First, mainstream news reporting was examined. Using Lexis-Nexis, all reports pertaining to Rathergate that appeared in *The New York Times* were collected for analysis. As Table A.1 shows, there were a relatively small number of reports dedicated to Rathergate, so each article was included in the research sample. The *New York Times* was an appropriate choice to assess mainstream media reporting because it has the highest circulation rate of any daily newspaper. Once all applicable newspaper articles had been collected, web logs were selected for analysis. Since there is no established method for determining what constitutes a prominent blog, the researcher used a criterion to rank blogs' relative influence based on the number of other blogs that link to them. While this might not be a perfect measure of influence, or even readership, it is a common measure found on two prominent online rankings: the *Blogstreet* "Blog Influence Quotient" (www.blogstreet.com) and the *Truth Laid Bear* "Ecosystem" (www.truthlaidbear.com).[2] In order to supplement these influence rankings, only widely read—at least by blogosphere standards—blogs that receive more than 100,000 average daily hits or page views were considered. Using these two points of reference, three blogs of varying political perspectives were chosen: Instapundit (libertarian), Eschaton (liberal), and

Power Line (conservative). The choice of Power Line merits further explanation because this particular blog did not appear on Blogstreet's ranking of influential blogs. In this instance, the researcher determined that Power Line's having previously been selected as *Time Magazine's* "Blog of the Year," combined with its considerable readership, were acceptable measures of its influence, even compared to other blogs deemed more significant in the online rankings.

Once each blog was selected, all postings pertaining to Rathergate were retrieved and saved into Microsoft Word documents. Because there is no repository for archived blog postings with customizable search options, the researcher read through all archived posts on each blog in order to make sure every entry related to Rathergate had been retrieved and placed into the research sample.[3] Table A.1 indicates that a total of 404 blog postings were acquired and analyzed for content. Although consideration was given to using a sampling of the total number of posts, this was ultimately deemed unnecessary given the informal nature of blog entries; posts can range in length from one word or phrase to several hundred words.

After all data were collected, QDA was used to analyze each of the 56 news reports and 404 blog posts. First, preliminary coding categories were established during a cursory read through of the entire sample. This was followed by a second, more thorough reading of each article and blog entry, accompanied by the development of a protocol design, which helped guide data collection by providing a standardized document containing information from related to emergent frames, as well as any contextual questions raised by the researcher during data analysis. Upon completion of this second phase, each protocol was reviewed and the preliminary coding categories were refined based on this more thorough review of the data. Finally, each document was read again along with another examination of each protocol to verify the accuracy of all identified frames, as well as the discourse that emerged during both scandals.

Table A.1. Distribution of articles and blog entries about the Rathergate for *The New York Times* and select web logs.

Scandal	The New York Times	Eschaton (Liberal)	Instapundit (Libertarian)	Power Line (Conservative)
Rathergate	56	40	206	158
TOTAL	59	42	210	189

CHAPTER 4: SUBVERTING OLD GOVERNMENT WITH NEW MEDIA: UNDERSTANDING THE WIKILEAKS EFFECT

Chapter 4 is primarily focused on media coverage of Julian Assange and WikiLeaks' brand of activist journalism. Data collection and analysis for this chapter therefore did not involve the examination of the WikiLeaks website and the leaked documents posted therein, but rather on the framing of WIki-Leaks in mainstream news reports. An initial search using *The New York Times* website yielded approximately 12,800 relevant "hits" pertaining to WikiLeaks. Similar to Chapter 3, *The New York Times* was determined to be an appropriate choice to analyze mainstream media reporting of WikiLeaks because it has the highest circulation rate of any daily newspaper and ranks as the fifth most popular news website (approximately 59,500,000 unique monthly visitors as of August 8, 2013) according to eBizMBA, which monitors news and corporate websites for e-Business purposes. Since WikiLeaks was founded in 2006, a second time-specific search was conducted with the parameters of January 1, 2005 and April 30, 2013; this returned 6770 results, with the earliest article published in February of 2008. Starting with a random number, every fortieth article was then added to the research sample. In the event that a selected article was not specifically about WikiLeaks or Julian Assange, or they were mentioned only in an ancillary fashion, it was removed from the sample and the next article on the list was selected as a replacement. Using this procedure, a final sample of 158 news reports was drawn for subsequent analysis.

Content analysis of all collected articles was completed using QDA. Each news report was first copied and saved as offline files and placed in chronological order for later analysis. An initial round of coding was completed in order to collect a preliminary list of relevant themes and organize an accurate timeline of events. Using a protocol design (see Altheide 1996), a second reading of each article was completed; preliminary coding categories were refined and then plotted using Freemind, an open-source mapping software. A final review of each document helped ensure the accuracy of identified frames. It should be noted that additional news sources were then used in order to collect relevant and compelling excerpts that contextualize the themes identified when coding articles published by *The New York Times*.

CHAPTER 5: CONNECTING THE WEB TO THE STREET: HYBRID SOCIAL MOVEMENTS AND ONLINE ADVOCACY NETWORKS

The purpose of this chapter is not so much to assess the content of claims published online by political activists as to gain insight on how social movement organizations (SMO) like the Tea Party are using the Internet's networking capacity as a vehicle to disseminate claims, communicate with advocates, attract supporters, promote activism, and obtain resources. The decision to use the Tea Party as a case study was due to the movement's success in combining grassroots operations with online claims-making and protest strategies. Deciding on the criteria for selecting appropriate Tea Party websites was a difficult process; normal sampling was impossible because there is no "master list" of all existing Tea Party sites (see Van Aelst and Walgrave 2002, 472). Using a more established national organization—the Tea Party Patriots—as a baseline, a link analysis model consisting of a cursory diagram of external links to other Tea Party websites was mapped. The hyperlinks connecting those national sites to additional Tea Party affiliated groups were then added to expand this model. Search engines were used to identify additional Tea Party web spaces, given that appearing prominently in search results could result in a greater likelihood of being *discovered* by prospective audiences.[4] Van Aelst and Walgrave (2002) suggest that this method of selection may manipulate the final results, thereby hindering findings related to the networking function of those websites; this is acknowledged as a potential problem. For this reason, the model diagrammed in Chapter 5 only contains general information and not the names of any specific organizations within the Tea Party. A generic model was deemed sufficient to illustrate the fluidity of an online advocacy network without the risk of inaccurately depicting the actual interconnectedness of specific Tea Party sites, since hyperlinks can easily be generated or removed, thereby reshaping the network.

A total of ten national Tea Party organization websites were examined for structure and content. Since many of these sites had links to social media outlets like Facebook, blogs, and regional Tea Party web spaces, which could be charted into the link analysis, the ten initial sites were deemed sufficient based on similar prior research (Van Aelst and Walgrave 2002). Because each website was not necessarily examined to assess the content of claims, a modified coding protocol was designed to categorize elements found on each site (e.g., hyperlinks to external sites, interactive elements, advertising of offline events, donations, etc.) into one concise document that could be used to draw conclusions about the function and purpose of the Tea Party online network. However, due to time constraints, the researcher's notes gathered when coding each individual site were not merged into a master protocol. Each website was reviewed a second time to verify the accuracy of the established codes, but the possibility exists that analytical errors might have occurred due to bypassing the development of a master protocol.

CHAPTER 6: FROM BACK ROOMS TO CYBER-LOBBIES: HOW THE NATIONAL RIFLE ASSOCIATION USES THE INTERNET TO MOBILIZE SUPPORT

This aim of chapter is very similar to that of Chapter 3 in that it is not designed to analyze the rhetorical content of claims; the purpose is to examine how online technology functions as a mobilizing structure for pressure groups and other political claimants. The decision to focus this chapter's case study on the National Rifle Association's (NRA) web presence was based on a general compatibility to Best's (1990) definition of insider claims-making. The NRA has amassed considerable support and resources; it also maintains a visible presence in American politics, which has helped the group gain a level of entrée with policymakers that typifies membership in the polity. As such, examination of the NRA web site was deemed a suitable case study.

Data for this chapter were acquired by content analyzing the structure and content of the NRA's primary site, affiliate web pages, and various social networking forums. This entailed examining the techniques used to mobilize support, such as online protest tactics, fundraising mechanisms, and so forth. Data collection and analysis were conducted in a manner similar to that of Chapter 3; likewise, a modified protocol design was not developed during the data analysis phase due to time constraints. However, the initial coding categories were entered into a Freemind mapping document. Upon a second review of each website included in the sample, codes were then collapsed according to two major themes: distribution of claims and mobilization tactics.

CHAPTER 7: ALL THE NEWS THAT'S FIT TO POST: BIG MEDIA AND THE SHIFT TO ONLINE COVERAGE

This chapter offers both an overview of media culture in an online world and an analysis of news presentation and interactivity on mass press websites. In order to assess the similarities in content and layout of online news coverage, websites were chosen from news organizations that have a national audience and use different offline formats to present news (e.g., print, radio, television): *The New York Times* maintains the largest circulation of any daily newspaper; Fox News Channel has the biggest audience of any 24-hour cable news network on television (Holcomb, Mitchell, and Rosenstiel 2012); and National Public Radio reaches approximately 35 million listeners each week by operating in partnership with more than 800 member radio stations (as of August 16, 2013; source: www.npr.org). From these sources, an analysis of each news agency's website was conducted in a manner similar to Chapter 5. Although data collection and analysis for this chapter were less empirically oriented than all of the other chapters, a QDA approach was nonetheless used to examine the unique structural characteristics of each website (e.g., hyper-linking, feedback loops, print reports, multimedia, interactive elements, and so forth).

NOTES

1. There was slight variation in method of analysis between chapters designed to explore the content of claims (chapters 3, 4, and 6) and those that examine the structure and purpose of websites (chapters 2 and 5).

2. It should be noted that the Blogstreet website, and by consequence the Blog Influence Quotient, is no longer active.

3. For the Rathergate scandal, archived posts were reviewed from September 8, 2004 (the day that Dan Rather's report on President Bush's military service aired), through March 31, 2005.

4. It is reasonable to assume that smaller, localized Tea Party sites are less likely to appear on the first page of search engine hits as compared with national organizations, but may nonetheless be easily located by audiences who are specifically searching online for groups operating in a specific jurisdiction or locale.

References

Abbey-Lambretz, Kate. 2013. "Biggby Coffee Terminates Michigan Teen Employee After 'Horrific' Trayvon Martin Tweet." *The Huffington Post*, July 18. Accessed August 1, 2013. http://www.huffingtonpost.com/2013/07/18/biggby-coffee-trayvon-martin-employee-tweet_n_3616768.html.

ABC News. 2007. "ABC News Joins Forces with Facebook." ABC News, December 18. Accessed November 14, 2012. http://abcnews.go.com/Technology/Politics/story?id=3899006&page=1#.UZbFXYI1fw4.

———. 2011. "ABC News, Yahoo! News Announce Online Alliance." ABC News, October 3. Accessed May 6, 2013. http://abcnews.go.com/US/abc-news-yahoo-news-announce-online-alliance/story?id=14650998#.UZVW_IL43w5.

Adorno, Theodor W. 1991. *The Culture Industry: Selected Essays on Mass Culture*. London: Routledge.

Altheide, David L. 1974. *Creating Reality: How TV News Distorts Events*. Beverly Hills, CA: Sage.

———. 1987. "Ethnographic Content Analysis." *Qualitative Sociology* 10:65–77.

———. 1992. "Gonzo Justice." *Symbolic Interaction* 15:69–86.

———. 1995. *An Ecology of Communication: Cultural Formats of Control*. Hawthorne, NY: Aldine de Gruyter.

———. 1996. *Qualitative Media Analysis*. Newbury Park, CA: Sage.

———. 2002. *Creating Fear: News and the Construction of Crisis*. Hawthorne, NY: Aldine de Gruyter.

———. 2004. "The Control Narrative of the Internet." *Symbolic Interaction* 27:232–45.

Altheide, David L., Barbara Gray, Roy Janisch, Lindsey Korbin, Ray Maratea, Debra Neill, Joseph Reaves, and Felicia Van Deman. 2001. "News Constructions of Fear and Victim: An Exploration Through Triangulated Qualitative Document Analysis." *Qualitative Inquiry* 7:304–22.

Altheide, David L. and R.S. Michalowski. 1999. "Fear in the News: A Discourse of Control." *The Sociological Quarterly* 40:475–503.

Altheide, David L. and Robert P. Snow. 1979. *Media Logic*. Beverly Hills, CA: Sage.

Apple, R.W., Jr. 1996. "25 Years Later: Lessons From the Pentagon Papers." *The New York Times*, June 23.

Arpaio, Joe and Len Sherman. 2008. *Joe's Law: America's Toughest Sheriff Takes on Illegal Immigration, Drugs, and Everything Else That Threatens America*. New York: AMACOM.

Associated Press. 2010. "Poll: Arpaio's Approval Rating Has Fallen." *The Arizona Republic*, January 26. Accessed January 2, 2012. http://www.azcentral.com/ /news/articles/2010/01/26/20100126arpaio-poll-approval-rating html.

———. 2013. "Alabama Man Charged with Murder After Fight over Movies." Fox News, May 11. Accessed May 13, 2013. http://www.foxnews.com/us/2013/05/11/alabama-man-charged-with-murder-after-fight-over-movies/.

Bagdikian, Ben H. 1997. *The Media Monopoly.* Boston: Beacon Press.

Baier, Bret. 2012. "What President Obama Really Said in That '60 Minutes' Interview About Benghazi." Fox News, November 5. Accessed April 16, 2013. http://politics.blogs.foxnews.com/2012/11/05/what-president-obama-really-said-60-minutes-interview-about-benghazi.

Barrett, Ted and Tom Cohen. 2013. "Senate Rejects Expanded Gun Background Checks." *CNN*, April 18. Accessed April 22, 2013. http://www.cnn.com/2013/04/17/politics/senate-guns-vote.

Batty, David. 2011. "Arab Spring Leads Surge in Events Captured on Cameraphones." *The Guardian*, December 29. Accessed October 22, 2012. http://www.guardian.co.uk/world/2011/dec/29/arab-spring-captured-on-cameraphones.

Baum, Matthew A. and Tim Groeling. 2008. "New Media and the Polarization of American Political Discourse." *Political Communication* 25:345–65.

BBC. 2012. "Malala Yousafzal: Portrait of a Girl Blogger." *BBC*, October 10. Accessed November 10, 2012. http://www.bbc.co.uk/news/magazine-19899540.

———. 2013. "Malala Yousafzal Leaves Queen Elizabeth Hospital." *BBC*, January 4. Accessed January 7, 2013. http://www.bbc.co.uk/news/uk-england-birmingham- 20908439.

Becker, Howard S. 1963. *Outsiders: Studies in the Sociology of Deviance.* New York: Free Press.

Beckett, Charlie and James Ball. 2012. *WikiLeaks: News in the Networked Era.* Malden, MA: Polity.

Beetham, Margaret. 2006. "Periodicals and the New Media: Women and Imagined Communities." *Women's Studies International Forum* 29:231–40.

Benford, Robert D. and David A. Snow. 2000. "Framing Processes and Social Movements: An Overview and Assessment." *Annual Review of Sociology* 26:611–39.

Bennett, W. Lance. 2005. *News: The Politics of Illusion.* New York: Pearson.

Berg, Bruce L. 2006. *Qualitative Research Methods for the Social Sciences (6th Edition).* Boston: Allyn and Bacon.

Berlo, David K., James B. Lemert, and Robert J. Mertz. 1969. "Dimensions for Evaluating the Acceptability of Message Sources." *Public Opinion Quarterly* 33:562-76.

Berman, Paul S. 2003. "The Internet Community Definition, and the Social Meaning of Legal Jurisdiction." In *Virtual Publics: Policy and Community in an Electronic Age*, edited by Beth E. Kolko, 49–82. New York: Columbia University Press.

Berns, Nancy. 2009. "Contesting the Victim Card: Closure Discourse and Emotion in Death Penalty Rhetoric." *The Sociological Quarterly* 50:383–406.

Best, Joel. 1990. *Threatened Children: Rhetoric and Concern About Child-Victims.* Chicago: University of Chicago Press.

———. 1995. *Images of Issues: Typifying Contemporary Social Problems.* Hawthorne, NY: Aldine de Gruyter.

———. 2008. *Social Problems.* New York: W.W. Norton.

Bjelopera, Jerome P., Erin Bagalman, Sarah W. Caldwell, Kristin M. Finklea, and Gail McCallion. 2013. *Public Mass Shootings in the United States: Selected Implications for Federal Public Health and Safety Policy.* Washington, DC: Congressional Research Service.

Black, Duncan. 2005. "What Liberal Media?" *Eschaton*, January 9. Accessed April 5, 2005. http://atrios.blogspot.com/2005_01_09_atrios_archive.html#1105408727093.

Bohm, Robert M. 2007. *Deathquest III: An Introduction to the Theory and Practice of Capital Punishment in the United States.* Cincinnati, OH: Anderson.

Bohm, Robert M., Ronald E. Vogel, and Albert A. Maisto. 1993. "Knowledge and Death Penalty Opinion: A Panel Study." *Journal of Criminal Justice* 21:29–45.

Boykoff, Jules, and Eulalie Laschever. 2011. "The Tea Party Movement, Framing, and the US Media." *Social Movement Studies* 10:341–66.

Broache, Anne. 2008. "Information Overload in the Facebook-ABC Presidential Debates?" CNET, January 6. Accessed November 14, 2012. http://news.cnet.com/8301-10784_3-9841291-7.html.

Brown, Phil. 1992. "Popular Epidemiology and Toxic Waste Contamination: Lay and Professional Ways of Knowing." *Journal of Health and Social Behavior* 35:34–52.

———. 1997. "Popular Epidemiology Revisited." *Current Sociology* 45:137–56.

Brown, Peter. 2013. *U.S. Voters Say Snowden Is Whistle-Blower, Not Traitor, Quinnipiac University National Poll Finds; Big Shift on Civil Liberties vs. Counter-Terrorism.* Hamden, CT: Quinnipiac University Polling Institute. Accessed August 16, 2013. http://www.quinnipiac.edu/images/polling/us/us07102013.pdf/.

Bumiller, Elisabeth. 2010. "Video Shows U.S. Killing of Reuters Employees." *The New York Times,* April 6.

Burns, John F. and Ravi Somaiya. 2010. "WikiLeaks Founder on the Run, Trailed by Notoriety." *The New York Times,* October 23.

Bureau of Labor Statistics. 2011. *Union Members—2010.* Washington, DC: U.S. Department of Labor.

Carter, Denise. 2005. "Living in Virtual Communities: An Ethnography of Human Relationships in Cyberspace." *Information, Communication, and Society* 8:148–67.

C-SPAN. 2012. "Cybersecurity Act of 2012 Motion to Proceed Continued." C-SPAN, July 26. Accessed March 16, 2013. http://www.c-spanvideo.org/appearance/602055849.

Carty, Victoria and Jake Onyett. 2006. "Protest, Cyberactivism and New Social Movements: The Reemergence of the Peace Movement Post 9/11." *Social Movement Studies* 5:229–49.

Castells, Manuel. 2009. *Communication Power.* New York: Oxford University Press.

Cavaliere, Victoria. 2013. "Ohio School District Votes to Allow Janitors to Carry Guns on Campus." *New York Daily News,* January 12. Accessed September 1, 2013. http://www.nydailynews.com/news/national/ohio-school-district-votes-arm-janitors-article-1.1238799.

CBS News. 2010a. "McConnell: WikiLeaks Head a High-Tech Terrorist." CBS News, December 5. Accessed February 22, 2013. http://www.cbsnews.com/2100-501707_162-7119787.html.

CBS News. 2010b. "Where America Stands: Issues Facing the Country (November 29-December 2, 2010)." CBS News, New York. Accessed February 22, 2013. http://www.cbsnews.com/stories/2010/12/03/politics/main7115593.shtml.

Center for Media and Public Affairs. 2012. *Study: Media Framed Benghazi in Obama's Terms.* Arlington, VA: The Center for Media and Public Affairs, Arlington, VA. Accessed April 18, 2013. http://www.cmpa.com/media_room_press_05_13_13.html.

Chadwick, Andrew. 2006. *Internet Politics: States, Citizens, and New Communication* Technologies. New York: Oxford University Press.

Chaiken, Meredith. 2010. "Poll: Americans Say WikiLeaks Harmed Public Interest; Most Want Assange Arrested." *The Washington Post,* December 14. Accessed March 8, 2013. http://www.washingtonpost.com/wp-dyn/content/article/2010/12/14/AR2010121401650_pf.html.

Chow, Denise. 2013. "Most Americans Blame Global Warming for Extreme Weather." NBC News, May 1. Accessed May 6, 2013. http://www.nbcnews.com/id/51735366/ns/technology_and_science-science/t/most-americans-blame-global-warming-extreme-weather/.

Clark, John D. and Nuno S. Themudo. 2006. "Linking the Web and the Street: Internet-Based "Dotcauses" and the 'Anti-Globalization' Movement." *World Development* 34:50–74.

CNN. 2012. "'Payola' Scandal Rocks CNN IReport's Citizen Journalist Platform." CNN, August 17. Accessed April 18, 2013. http://ireport.cnn.com/docs/DOC-829981.

———. 2013. "Sources: Possible Suspects Sought in Boston Blasts." CNN, April 17. Accessed April 24, 2013. http://news.blogs.cnn.com/2013/04/17/source-arrest-made-in-boston-bombing/.

Colbert, Stephen. 2005. "The Word - Truthiness." *The Colbert Report,* October 17. Accessed December 4, 2012. http://www.colbertnation.com/the-colbert-report-videos/24039/october-17-2005/the-word---truthiness.

Collins, Randall. 1981. "On the Microfoundations of Macrosociology." *The American Journal of Sociology* 86:984–1014.

Connelly, Joel. 2013. "Fox News Host: 'Punch' Obama Voters 'in the Face'." *Seattle Post-Intelligencer*, May 24. Accessed May 26, 2013. http://blog.seattlepi.com/seattlepolitics/2013/05/24/fox-news-host-punch-obama-voters-in-the-face/.

Couch, Carl J. 1984. *Constructing Civilizations*. Greenwich, CT: JAI Press.

Crouch, Ian. 2013. "Marco Rubio's Water-Bottle Moment." *The New Yorker*, February 13. Accessed September 8, 2013. http://www.newyorker.com/online/blogs/newsdesk/2013/02/marco-rubio-water-bottle-moment.html.

Davis, H.P. 1974. "The Early History of Broadcasting in the United States." In *The Radio Industry: The Story of Its Development*, 189–225. New York: Arno Press.

DeFleur, Melvin L. 1966. *Theories of Mass Communication*. New York: David McKay.

DeFleur, Melvin L. and Sandra Ball-Rokeach. 1975. *Theories of Mass Communication*. New York: David McKay.

DeMarban, Alex. 2013. "Nation's First Civilian Drones Set to Take Flight over Alaska." *Alaska Dispatch*, August 7. Accessed September 8, 2013. http://www.alaskadispatch.com/article/20130807/nations-first-civilian-drones-set-take-flight-over-alaska.

Dennis, Kingsley. 2008 "*Keeping a Close Watch*—The Rise of Self-Surveillance and the Threat of Digital Exposure. *The Sociological Review* 56:347–57.

Diani, Mario. 2003. "Introduction: Social Movements, Contentious Actions, and Social Networks: 'From Metaphor to Substance'?" In *Social Movements and Networks: Relational Approaches to Collective Action*, edited by Mario Diani and Doug McAdam, 1-18. Oxford: Oxford University Press.

DiMaggio, Paul, Eszter Hargittai, W. Russell Neuman, and John P. Robinson. 2001. "Social Implications of the Internet." *Annual Review of Sociology* 27:307–36.

Dionne, E.J. 2012. "The Party Movement Is Dead." *Real Clear Politics*, October 25. Accessed November 8, 2012. www.realclearpolitics.com/articles/2012/10/25/tea_party_movement_is_dead_115916.html.

Domscheit-Berg, Daniel. 2011. *Inside WikiLeaks: My Time with Julian Assange at the World's Most Dangerous Website*. New York: Crown Publishers.

Downs, Anthony. 1972. "Up and Down with Ecology—the 'Issue-Attention Cycle.'" *The Public Interest* 28:38–50.

Doyle, Aaron. 2003. *Arresting Images: Crime and Policing in Front of the Television Camera*. Toronto: University of Toronto Press.

Duwe, Grant. 2007. *Mass Murder in the United States: A History*. Jefferson, NC: McFarland.

Ellsworth, Phoebe and Samuel Gross. 1994. "Hardening of the Attitudes: Americans' Views of the Death Penalty." *Journal of Social Issues* 50:19-52.

Emery, Edwin, Phillip H. Ault, and Warren K. Agee. 1973. *Introduction to Mass Communications*. New York: Dodd, Mead & Company.

Engel, Richard. 2012. "The Arab Spring Is Dead – And Syria Is Writing Its Obituary." NBC News, September 7. Accessed October 16, 2012. http://worldnews.nbcnews.com/_news/2012/09/07/13686562-the-arab-spring-is-dead-and-syria-is-writing-its-obituary.

Ericson, Richard V., Patricia M. Baranek, and Janet B.L. Chan. 1989. *Negotiating Control: A Study of News Sources*. Toronto: University of Toronto Press.

Eveland, William P., Jr. 2003. "A "Mix of Attributes" Approach to the Study of Media Effects and New Communication Technologies." *Journal of Communication* 53:395–410.

Fallows, Deborah and Lee Rainie. 2004. *The Internet as a Unique News Source: Millions Go Online for News and Images Not Covered in the Mainstream Press*. Washington, D.C.: Pew Research Center.

Farber, David. 1988. *Chicago '68*. Chicago: University of Chicago Press.

Fishel, Justin. 2010. "Military Raises Questions About Credibility of Leaked Iraq Shooting Video." Fox News, April 7. Accessed March 1, 2013. http://www.foxnews.com/politics/2010/04/07/military-raises-questions-credibility-leaked-Iraq-shooting-video/.

Fishman, Mark. 1980. *Manufacturing the News*. Austin, TX: University of Texas Press.

Fishman, Mark and Gray Cavender. 1998. *Entertaining Crime: Television Reality Programs*. Hawthorne, NY: Aldine de Gruyter.

Follman, Mark. 2013. "New Research Confirms Gun Rampages Are Rising—and Armed Civilians Don't Stop Them." *Mother Jones*, April 11. Accessed April 16, 2013. http://www.motherjones.com/politics/2013/04/mass-shootings-rampages-rising-data.

Follman, Mark, Gavin Aronsen, and Deanna Pan. 2012. "A Guide to Mass Shootings in America." *Mother Jones*, July 20. Accessed March 22, 2013. http://www.motherjones.com/politics/2012/07/mass-shootings-map.

Foucault, Michel. (1975) 1995. *Discipline & Punish: The Birth of the Prison*. New York: Vintage Books.

Fox News. 2010. "Media Bias: Then and Now." *Fox & Friends*, April 3.

———. 2013. "White House Gearing Up for War on Affordable Energy?" Fox News, March 4. Accessed March 23, 2013. http://video.foxnews.com/v/2203074038001/white-house-gearing-up-for-war-on-affordable-energy/.

Frankel, Max. 1996. "Top Secret: No One Is Heeding the Lessons the Pentagon Papers Still Teach." *The New York Times*, June 16.

Friedman, Emily. 2010. "BP Buys 'Oil' Search Terms to Redirect Users to Official Company Website." ABC News, June 5. Accessed January 2, 2013. http://abcnews.go.com/Technology/bp-buys-search-engine-phrases-redirecting-users/story?id=10835618.

Frumin, Aliyah. 2012. "Rep. McCarthy: Conversation About Gun Control 'Has to Go Forward.'" *MSNBC*, December 14. Accessed March 17, 2013. http://tv.msnbc.com/2012/12/14/rep-mccarthy-conversation-about-gun-control-has-to-go-forward/.

Gainor, Dan. 2013 "Liberal Media Spin Benghazi Scandal to Protect Team Obama." Fox News, May 9. Accessed May 12, 2013. http://www.foxnews.com/opinion/2013/05/09/liberal-media-spin-benghazi-scandal-to-protect-team-obama/.

Gans, Herbert J. 1979. *Deciding What's News*. New York: Pantheon.

Gatson, Sarah N. and Amanda Zweerink. 2004. "Ethnography Online: 'Natives' Practicing and Inscribing Community." *Qualitative Research* 4:179–200.

Gayle, Damien. 2013. "UK Government Plans to Track ALL Web Use: MI5 to Install 'Black Box' Spy Devices to Monitor British Internet Traffic." *Daily Mail*, February 6. Accessed May 18, 2013. http://www.dailymail.co.uk/sciencetech/article-2274388/MI5-install-black-box-spy-devices-monitor-UK-internet-traffic.html.

Gellman, Barton and Jerry Markon. 2013. "Edward Snowden Says Motive Behind Leaks Was to Expose 'Surveillance State.'" *Washington Post*, June 10. Accessed September 6, 2013. http://www.washingtonpost.com/politics/edward-snowden-says-motive-behind-leaks-was-to-expose-surveillance-state/2013/06/09/aa3f0804-d13b-11e2-a73e-826d299ff459_story.html.

Giles, David. 2006. "Constructing Identities in Cyberspace: The Case of Eating Disorders." *British Journal of Social Psychology* 45:463–77.

Gitlin, Todd. 1980. *The Whole World Is Watching*. Berkeley, CA: University of California Press.

Gladwell, Malcolm. 2010. "Small Change: Why the Revolution Will Not Be Tweeted." *The New Yorker*, October 4. Accessed February 2, 2013. http://www.newyorker.com/reporting/2010/10/04/101004fa_fact_gladwell.

Glassner, Barry. 1999. *The Culture of Fear*. New York: Basic Books.

Glater, Jonathan D. 2005. "Keeping CBS's Eye on Its Own World." *The New York Times*, January 15.

Gleick, James. 2011. *The Information: A History, a Theory, a Flood*. New York: Pantheon.

Gold, Matea, Joseph Tanfani, and Lisa Mascaro. 2012. "NRA Clout Rooted More in Its Tactics Than Its Election Spending." *The Los Angeles Times*, July 29. Accessed March 10, 2013. http://articles.latimes.com/2012/jul/29/nation/la-na-nra-clout-20120729.

Goode, Luke. 2009. "Social News, Citizen Journalism and Democracy." *New Media & Society* 11:1287–1305.

Graber, Doris A. 1988. *Processing the News*. White Plains, NY: Longman.

Granovetter, Mark S. 1973. "The Strength of Weak Ties." *American Journal of Sociology* 78:1360–80.

Greenberg, Alan. 2012. "WikiLeaks Tightens Ties to Anonymous in Leak of Stratfor Emails." *Forbes*, February 27. Accessed March 8, 2013. http://www.forbes.com/sites/andygreenberg/2012/02/27/wikileaks-tightens-ties-to-anonymous-in-leak-of-stratfor-emails/.

Griffin, Marie L. 2001. *The Use of Force by Detention Officers*. El Paso, TX: LFB Scholarly Publishing.

Grinberg, Emanuella. 2012. "Hasbro to Unveil Black and Silver Easy-Bake Oven After Teen's Petition." *CNN*, December 18. Accessed April 3, 2013. http://www.cnn.com/2012/12/18/living/hasbro-easy-bake-oven.

Grossman, Lev. 2004. "Meet Joe Blog." *Time*, June 13. Accessed August, 14, 2011. http://content.time.com/time/magazine/article/0,9171,650732,00.html.

The Guardian. 2011. "Julian Assange and WikiLeaks: No Case, No Need." *The Guardian*, September 2. Accessed February 18. http://www.guardian.co.uk/commentisfree/2011/sep/02/leader-wikileaks-unredacted-release.

Gurevitch, Michael, Stephen Coleman, and Jay G. Blumler. 2009. "Political Communication—Old and New Media Relationships." *The Annals of the American Academy of Political and Social Science* 625:164–81.

Halliday, Josh. 2011. "London Riots: How BlackBerry Messenger Played a Key Role." *The Guardian*, August 8. Accessed August 12, 2012. http://www.guardian.co.uk/media/2011/aug/08/london-riots-facebook-twitter-blackberry.

Hargittai, Eszter. 2004. "Internet Access and Use in Context." *New Media and Society* 6:137–43.

Harmon, Amy. 2004. "The Struggle for Iraq: The Internet; New Technology Loosens Control over Images of War." *The New York Times*, May 14.

The Hartford Courant. 2013. "Senate Votes Down Background Check Expansion." *The Hartford Courant*, April 17. Accessed April 18, 2013. http://www.courant.com/news/breaking/hc-gun-vote-fail-0418-20130417,0,2900674.story.

Heisbourg, François. 2011. "Leaks and Lessons." *Survival* 53(1):207–16.

Hepburn, John R. and Marie L. Griffin. 1998. *Jail Recidivism in Maricopa County: A Report Submitted to the Maricopa County's Sheriff Office*. Tempe, AZ: Arizona State University.

Hilgartner, Stephen and Charles L. Bosk. 1988. "The Rise and Fall of Social Problems: A Public Arenas Model." *The American Journal of Sociology* 94:53–78.

Hinderaker, John H. 2004. "Suicide Bombers and CBS News" *Power Line*, September 12. Accessed December 5, 2006. http://powerlineblog.com/archives/007807.php.

Hine, Christine. 2000. *Virtual Ethnography*. London: Sage Publications.

Hirsch, Paul M. 1972. "Processing Fads and Fashions: An Organization-Set Analysis of Cultural Industry Systems." *The American Journal of Sociology* 77:639–59.

Hitchens, Christopher. 2010. "Turn Yourself In, Julian Assange: The WikiLeaks Founder Is an Unscrupulous Megalomaniac with a Political Agenda." *Slate*, December 6. Accessed March 3, 2013. www.slate.com/articles/news_and_politics/fighting_words/2010/12/turn_yourself_in_julian_assange.html.

Hochschild, Arlie Russell. 1979. "Emotion Work, Feeling Rules, and Social Structure." *American Journal of Sociology* 85:551–74.

Hoffman, Lindsay H. 2006. "Is Internet Content Different After All? A Content Analysis of Mobilizing Information in Online and Print Newspapers." *Journalism & Mass Communication Quarterly* 83:58–76.

Hofstadter, Richard. 1963. *Anti-Intellectualism in American Life*. New York: Alfred A. Knopf.

Holcomb, Jesse, Amy Mitchell, and Tom Rosenstiel. 2012. "Cable: By the Numbers" in *The State of the News Media 2013*. Washington, D.C.: The Pew Research Center's Project for Excellence in Journalism, Pew Research Center. Accessed August 16, 2013. http://stateofthemedia.org/2012/cable-cnn-ends-its-ratings-slide-fox-falls-again/cable-by-the-numbers/.

Horkheimer, Max and Theodor W. Adorno. 1972. *Dialectic of Enlightenment*. New York: Herder and Herder.

Howard, Philip N. 2002. "Network Ethnography and the Hypermedia Organization: New Media, New Organizations, New Methods." *New Media and Society* 4:550–74.

Hunt, Kasie. 2013. "NRA Threatens to Punish Lawmakers on Gun Control Vote Despite Deal." *NBC News*, April 10. Accessed April 12, 2013. http://nbcpolitics.nbcnews.com/_news/2013/04/10/17694499-nra-threatens-to-punish-lawmakers-on-gun-control-vote-despite-deal.

Hurley, Anna L., Paul Sullivan, and John McCarthy. 2007. "The Construction of Self in Online Support Groups for Victims of Domestic Violence." *British Journal of Social Psychology* 46:859–74.

Ibarra, Peter R. and John I. Kitsuse. 2003. "Claims-Making Discourse and Vernacular Resources." In *Challenges and Choices: Constructionist Perspectives on Social Problems*, edited by James A. Holstein and Gale Miller, 17–50. Hawthorne, NY: Aldine de Gruyter.

Ingram, David. 2012. "Gun Control Movement Tries to Shed Election Losing Reputation." *Reuters,* December 15. Accessed March 29, 2013. http://www.reuters.com/article/2012/12/16/us-usa-shooting-public-opinion-idUSBRE8BF01L20121216.

Iyengar, Shanto and Donald R. Kinder. 1987. *News That Matters.* Chicago: University of Chicago Press.

Jacobe, Dennis. 2013. *Americans Want More Emphasis on Solar, Wind, Natural Gas.* Washington, DC: Gallup. Accessed April 14, 2013. http://www.gallup.com/poll/161519/americans-emphasis-solar-wind-natural-gas.aspx.

Jacobs, Ronald N. 2000. *Race, Media and the Crisis of Civil Society.* Cambridge, UK: Cambridge University Press.

Jamieson, Alastair. 2010. "Girl, 14, Fears 21,000 Party Guests After Facebook Invite Blunder." *The Telegraph*, September 20. Accessed October 18, 2012. http://www.telegraph.co.uk/technology/facebook/8012043/Girl-14-fears-21000-party-guests-after-Facebook-invite-blunder.html.

Jewett, Frank B. 1974. "The Development and Use of Radio Telephony as a Means of Communication." In *The Radio Industry: The Story of Its Development*, 114-39. New York: Arno Press.

Johnson, Thomas J., Barbara K. Kaye, Shannon L. Bichard, and W. Joann Wong. 2007. "Every Blog Has Its Day: Politically-Interested Internet Users' Perceptions of Blog Credibility." *Journal of Mediated Communication* 13:100–22.

Jones, Jeffrey M. 2010. *Americans Prioritize Energy over Environment for First Time.* Washington, DC: Gallup. Accessed April 16, 2013. http://www.gallup.com/poll/127220/americans-prioritize-energy-environment-first-time.aspx.

Katz, Elihu. 1992. "The End of Journalism? Notes on Watching the War." *Journal of Communication* 42:5–13.

Katz, James E. and Ronald E. Rice. 2002. *Social Consequences of Internet Use: Access, Involvement, and Interaction.* Cambridge, MA: MIT Press.

Keck, Margaret E. and Kathryn Sikkink. 1998. *Activists Beyond Borders: Advocacy Networks in International Politics.* Ithaca: Cornell University Press.

Klandermans, Bert and Dirk Oegema. 1987. "Potentials, Networks, Motivations and Barriers: Steps Toward Participation in Social Movements." *American Sociological Review* 52:519–31.

Klapper, Joseph T. 1960. *The Effects of Mass Communication.* New York: Free Press.

Klotz, Robert J. 2007. "Internet Campaigning for Grassroots and Astroturf Support." *Social Science Computer Review* 25:3–12.

Kopytoff, Verne G. 2011. "Blogs Wane as the Young Drift to Sites Like Twitter." *The New York Times*, February 21.

Kornblut, Anne E., Katharine Q. Seelye, and David D. Kirkpatrick. 2006. "Papers Knew of Foley E-Mail But Did Not Publish Articles." *The New York Times*, October 3.

Krattenmaker, Thomas G. and Powe, Lucas A., Jr. 1994. *Regulatory Broadcast Programming.* Cambridge and Washington, D.C.: MIT Press and AEI Press.

Krugman, Paul. 2012. "'This Tribal Nation." *The New York Times*, February 27. Accessed March 26, 2012. http://www.krugman.blogs.nytimes.com/2012/02/27/this-tribal-nation.

Kurtz, Howard. 1998. *Spin Cycle.* New York: Touchstone Books.

Ladurantaye, Steve. 2013. "CNN Learns from Newtown, Reports on Boston Bombing with 'Abundance of Caution'." *The Globe and Mail*, April 16. Accessed April 18, 2013. http://

www.theglobeandmail.com/news/world/cnn-learns-from-newtown-reports-on-boston-bombing-with-abundance-of-caution/article11265971/.

Ladyman, James. 2002. *Understanding Philosophy of Science*. New York: Routledge.

Leibowitz, Barry. 2011. "Facebook Blunder Invites 15,000 to Teen's 16th Birthday Party; 100 Cops Show Up, Too." CBS News, June 7. Accessed October 16, 2012. http://www.cbsnews.com/8301-504083_162-20069457-504083.html.

Leigh, David and Luke Harding. 2011. *WikiLeaks: Inside Julian Assange's War on Secrecy*. New York: PublicAffairs.

Levinson, Paul. 1999. *Digital McLuhan: A Guide to the Information Millennium*. New York: Routledge.

Lewis, Tom. 1992. "'A Godlike Presence': The Impact of Radio on the 1920s and 1930s." *Magazine of History* 6:26–33.

Lillis, Mike. 2013. "Rep. McCarthy, Mayor Bloomberg Cheer Manchin-Toomey Gun Bill." *The Hill*, April 10. Accessed April 17, 2013. http://thehill.com/blogs/blog-briefing-room/news/293031-rep-mccvarthy-mayor-bloomberg-cheer-mnchin-toomey-gun-bill.

Lord, Charles G., Lee Ross, and Mark R. Lepper. 1979. "Biased Assimilation and Attitude Polarization: The Effects of Prior Theories on Subsequently Considered Evidence." *Journal of Personality and Social Psychology* 37:2098-2109.

Loseke, Donileen R. 2000. "Ethos, Pathos, and Social Problems." *Social Problems* 12:41–54.

———. 2003. "Constructing Conditions, People, Morality, and Emotion: Expanding the Agenda of Constructionism." In *Challenges & Choices: Constructionist Perspectives on Social Problems*, edited by James A. Holstein and Gale Miller, 120–29. Hawthorne, NY: Aldine de Gruyter.

Lundman, Richard J. 2003. "The Newsworthiness and Selection Bias in News About Murder: Comparative and Relative Effects of Novelty and Race and Gender Typifications on Newspaper Coverage of Homicide." *Sociological Forum* 18:357–386.

Maag, Christopher. 2007. "Internet Hoax That Turned Fatal Draws Anger But No Charges." *The New York Times*, November 28. Accessed November 20, 2011. http://www.nytimes.com/2007/11/28/world/americas/28iht-28hoax.8508834.html.

MacAskill, Ewen. 2010. "Julian Assange Like a Hi-Tech Terrorist, Says Joe Biden." *The Guardian*, December 19. Accessed February 24, 2013. http://www.guardian .co.uk/media/2010/dec/19/assange-high-tech-terrorist-biden.

Mackey, Robert. 2010. "'Operation Payback' Attacks Target MasterCard and PayPal Sites to Avenge WikiLeaks." *The New York Times*, December 8. Accessed February 25, 2013. http://thelede.blogs.nytimes.com/2010/12/08/operation-payback-targets-mastercard-and-paypal-sites-to-avenge-wikileaks/.

MacKuen, Michael B. and Steven L. Coombs. 1981. *More Than News: Media Power in Public Affairs*. Beverly Hills, CA: Sage.

Madison, Lucy. 2012. "Richard Mourdock: Even Pregnancy from Rape Something 'God Intended.'" CBS News, October 23. Accessed May 24, 2013. www.cbsnews.com/8301-250_162-57538757/richard-mourdock-even-pregnancy-from-rape-something-god-intended/.

Mandell, Nina. 2011. "1500 People Show Up for 16-Year-Old's Birthday Party After She Forgets to Set Facebook Settings." *New York Daily News*, June 5. Accessed October 16, 2012. http://articles.nydailynews.com/2011-06-05/news/29645215_1_birthday-party-birthday-girl-privacy-settings.

Manjoo, Farhad. 2008. *True Enough: Learning to Live in a Post-Fact Society*. Hoboken, NJ: Wiley.

Maratea, R.J., and Philip R. Kavanaugh. 2012. "Deviant Identity in Online Contexts: New Directives in the Study of a Classic Concept." *Sociology Compass* 6:102–12.

Maratea, R.J. and Brian Monahan. 2013. "Crime Control as Mediated Spectacle: The Institutionalization of Gonzo Rhetoric in Modern Media and Politics." *Symbolic Interaction* 36:261–74.

Maratea, Ray. 2008. "The e-Rise and Fall of Social Problems: The Blogosphere as a Public Arena." *Social Problems* 55:139–60.

Marcuse, Herbert. (1964) 1991. *One-Dimensional Man: Studies in the Ideology of Advanced Industrial Society*. Boston: Beacon Press.

Martin, Roland. 2012. "America Should See the Newtown Carnage." CNN, December 23. Accessed August 18, 2013. http://www.cnn.com/2012/12/22/opinion/martin-newtown-carnage/index.html.

Martinez, Michael and Dave Alsup. 2013. "Mississippi Politician Urges Gunmakers in Connecticut, Elsewhere to Relocate." CNN, February 23. Accessed August 18, 2013. http://www.cnn.com/2013/02/22/us/mississippi-gunmakers-invite/index.html.

Mayer, Robert N. 2007. "Winning the War of Words: The "Front Group" Label in Contemporary Consumer Politics." *The Journal of American Culture* 30:96-109.

McAdam, Doug. 1996. "Conceptual Origins, Current Problems, Future Directions." In *Comparative Perspectives on Social Movements*, edited by Doug McAdam, John D. McCarthy, and Mayer N. Zald, 23-40. New York: Cambridge University Press.

———. 2003. "Beyond Structural Analysis: Toward a More Dynamic Understanding of Social Movements." In *Social Movements and Networks: Relational Approaches to Collective Action*, edited by Mario Diani and Doug McAdam, 281–98. New York: Oxford University Press.

McAdam, Doug and Ronnelle Paulsen. 1993. "Specifying the Relationship Between Social Ties and Activism." *American Journal of Sociology* 99:640–67.

McCarthy, John D. and Mayer N. Zald. 1977. "Resource Mobilization and Social Movements: A Partial Theory." *American Journal of Sociology* 82:121–41.

McCombs, Maxwell. 2004. *Setting the Agenda: The Mass Media and Public Opinion*. Cambridge, UK: Polity.

McLuhan, Marshall. 1960. *Explorations in Communication*. Boston: Beacon Press.

———. 1964. *Understanding Media: Extensions of Man*. New York: McGraw-Hill.

Melkote, Srinivas R. and H. Leslie Steeves. 2001. *Communication for Development in the Third World: Theory and Practice for Empowerment*, 2ⁿᵈ ed. Thousand Oaks, CA: Sage.

Meyer, David S. 2007. *The Politics of Protest: Social Movements in America*. New York: Oxford University Press.

Meyer, Dick. 2009. ""The Truth of Truthiness." CBS News, December 12. Accessed February 14, 2012. http://www.cbsnews.com/stories/2006/12/12/opinion/meyer/main2250923.html.

Meyrowitz, Joshua. 1985. *No Sense of Place: The Impact of Electronic Media on Social Behaviour*. New York: Oxford University Press.

———. 1994. "Medium Theory." In *Communication Theory Today*, edited by David Crowley and David Mitchell, 50–77. Stanford, CA: Stanford University Press.

Miller, Sunlen. 2013. "Senate Democrats Drop Assault Weapons Ban from Gun Bill." *ABC News*, March 19. Accessed March 20, 2013. http://abcnews.go.com/blogs/politics/2013/03/senate-democrats-drop-assault-weapons-ban-from-gun-bill/.

Mitchell, Amy, Tom Rosentiel, and Leah Christian. 2012. "Mobile Devices and News Consumption: Some Good Signs for Journalism" in *The State of the News Media 2012*. Washington, D.C.: The Pew Research Center's Project for Excellence in Journalism, Pew Research Center. Accessed February 13, 2013. http://stateofthemedia.org/2012/mobile-devices-and-news-consumption-some-good-signs-for-journalism/.

Monahan, Brian A. 2010. *The Shock of the News: Media Coverage and the Making of 9/11*. New York: NYU Press.

Monahan, Brian A. and R.J. Maratea. 2013. "Breaking News on *Nancy Grace*: Violent Crime in the Media." 209–27 in *Making Sense of Social Problems: New Images, New Issues*, edited by Joel Best and Scott R. Harris. Boulder, CO: Lynne Rienner.

Mooney, Chris. 2012. ""The Ugly Delusions of the Educated Conservative." *Salon*, February 24. Accessed March 26, 2012. www.salon.com/2012/02/24/the_ugly_delusions_of_the_educated_conservative/.

Mooney, Christopher Z. 1999. "The Politics of Morality Policy: Symposium Editor's Introduction." *Policy Studies Journal* 27:675–80.

Mooney, Christopher Z. and Mei-Hsien Lee. 1999. "The Temporal Diffusion of Morality Policy: The Case of Death Penalty Legislation in the American States." *Policy Studies Journal* 27:766–80.

Moore, Andy. 2011. "Riots in Tottenham After Mark Duggan Shooting Protest." *BBC*, August 7. Accessed August 12, 2012. http://www.bbc.co.uk/news/uk-england-london-14434318.

Morozov, Evgeny. 2011. *The Net Delusion: The Dark Side of Internet Freedom.* New York: PublicAffairs.

Morris, Nigel, Oliver Wright, and Adam Sherwin. 2011. "Government Could Censor Internet in Any Future Civil Unrest." *Belfast Telegraph*, August 12. Accessed August 12, 2012. http://www.belfasttelegraph.co.uk/news/local-national/uk/government-could-censor-internet-in-any-future-civil-unrest-28645760.html.

MSNBC. 2008. "'Hardball with Chris Matthews' for Friday, October 17, 2008." MSNBC, October 17. Accessed May 18, 2013. http://www.nbcnews.com/id/27297028/ns/msnbc-hardball_with_chris_matthews/t/hardball-chris-matthews-friday-october/#.Ua1_u7_3DjA.

———. 2011. "'The Rachel Maddow Show' for Friday, January 28, 2011." MSNBC, January 28. Accessed October 16, 2012. http://www.nbcnews.com/id/41351005/ns/msnbc-rachel_maddow_show/t/rachel-maddow-show-friday-january-th/#.UZbBgII1fw4.

Mungin, Lateef. 2013. "NRA Chief: Obama Makes 'Mockery' of American Freedoms." *CNN*, January 28. Accessed March 22, 2013. http://www.cnn.com/2013/01/23/politics/nra-response.

Newport, Frank. 2009. *Americans: Economy Takes Precedence Over Environment.* Washington, DC: Gallup. Accessed April 16, 2013. http://www.gallup.com/poll/116962/americans-economy-takes-precedence-environment.aspx.

———. 2013. *Americans Disapprove of Government Surveillance Programs.* Washington, DC: Gallup. Accessed August 8, 2013. http://www.gallup.com/poll/163043/americans-disapprove-government-surveillance-programs.aspx.

Nip, Joyce Y. M. 2004. "The Queer Sisters and Its Electronic Bulletin Board: A Study of the Internet for Social Movement Mobilization." *Information, Communication & Society* 7:23–49.

Niven, David. 2002. "Bolstering an Illusory Majority: The Effects of the Media's Portrayal of Death Penalty Support." *Social Science Quarterly* 83:671–89.

NM Insight. 2012. "Buzz in the Blogosphere: Millions More Bloggers and Blog Readers." NM Insight, March 8. Accessed November 8, 2012. http://nmincite.com/tag/blogs/.

Nocera, Joe. 2012. "Hacking General Petraeus." *The New York Times*, November 17.

Norris, Pippa. 2001. *Digital Divide: Civic Engagement, Information Poverty and the Internet in Democratic Societies.* New York: Cambridge University Press.

Pace, Gina. 2010. "WikiLeaks Distances Itself from Hackers – Somewhat." CBS News, December 9. Accessed March 11, 2013. http://cbsnews.com/8301-503543_162-20025147-503543.html.

Paolillo, John C. 1999. "The Virtual Speech Community: Social Network and Language Variation in IRC." *Journal of Computer-Mediated Communication* 4. Accessed August 27, 2008. http://jcmc.indiana.edu/vol4/issue4/paolillo.html.

Papacharissi, Zizi. 2004. "Democracy Online: Civility, Politeness, and the Democratic Potential of Online Political Discussion Groups." *New Media & Society* 6:259–83.

Park, Hun Myoung and James L. Perry. 2008. "Do Campaign Web Sites Really Matter in Electoral Civic Engagement? Empirical Evidence from the 2004 Post-Election Internet Tracking Survey." *Social Science Computer Review* 26:190–212.

Passy, Florence. 2003. "Social Networks Matter. But How?" In *Social Movements and Networks: Relational Approaches to Collective Action*, edited by Mario Diani and Doug McAdam, 21–48. Oxford: Oxford University Press.

Pearce, Matt. 2012. "2012 Is Tragic, but Mass Shootings Not Increasing, Experts Say." *Los Angeles Times*, December 18. Accessed May 29, 2013. http://articles.latimes.com/2012/dec/18/nation/la-na-nn-mass-shootings-common-20121218.

Peat, Don. 2010. "Cellphone Cameras Making Everyone a Walking Newsroom." *Toronto Sun*, February 1. Accessed October 18, 2012. http://www.torontosun.com/news/canada/2010/02/01/12693856.html.

Pein, Corey. 2005. "Blog-Gate." *Columbia Journalism Review* 43:30–35.

Peralta, Eyder. 2011. "Sen. Jon Kyl Corrects Erroneous Statement on Planned Parenthood." NPR, April 22. Accessed May 24, 2013. http://www.npr.org/blogs/thetwo-way/2011/04/22/135641326/sen-jon-kyl-corrects-erroneous-statement-on-planned-parenthood.

Perez, Victor W. 2013. "The Movement Linking Vaccines to Autism: Parents and the Internet." In *New Images, New Issues: Making Sense of Social Problems*, edited by Joel Best and Scott R. Harris, 71-89. Boulder, CO: Lynne Rienner.

Pew Research Center. 2007a. *Internet News Audience Highly Critical of News Organizations: Views of Press Values and Performance: 1985-2007*. Washington, DC, Pew Research Center for the People & the Press, Pew Research Center. Accessed May 14, 2012 http://people-press.org/reports/pdf/348.pdf.

———. 2007b. *The State of the News Media 2007. An Annual Report on American Journalism*. Washington, DC: The Pew Research Center's Project for Excellence in Journalism, Pew Research Center. Accessed May 14, 2012. http://www.stateofthenewsmedia.org/2007/.

———. 2011. *Beyond Red vs. Blue: The Political Ideology*. Washington, DC: Pew Research Center for the People & the Press, Pew Research Center. Accessed April 15, 2013. http://www.people-press.org/2011/05/04/beyond-red-vs-blue-the-political-typology/.

———. 2013a. *Benghazi Investigation Does Not Reignite Broad Public Interest*. Washington, DC: Pew Research Center for the People & the Press, Pew Research Center. Accessed April 15, 2013. http://www.people-press.org/2013/05/13/benghazi-investigation-does-not-reignite-broad-public-interest/.

———. 2013b. *The State of the News Media 2013. An Annual Report on American Journalism*. Washington, DC: Project for Excellence in Journalism, Pew Research Center. Accessed April 15, 2013. http://www.stateofthenewsmedia.org/2013/overview-5/.

Phillips, Michael M. 2009. "FreedomWorks Harnesses Growing Activism on the Right." *The Wall Street Journal*, October 5. Accessed January 25, 2013. http://online.wsj.com/article/SB125469984687962987.html.

Prior, Markus. 2005. "News vs. Entertainment: How Increasing Media Choice Widens Gaps in Political Knowledge and Turnout." *American Journal of Political Science* 49:577–92.

Public Policy Polling. 2011. *Arizona Voters Unhappy with Brewer on Redistricting*. Raleigh, NC: Public Policy Polling. Accessed January 8, 2012. http://www.publicpolicypolling.com/pdf/2011/PPP_Release_AZ_1122.pdf.

Rainie, Lee, Aaron Smith, Kay Lehman Schlozman, Henry Brady, and Sidney Verba. 2012. *Social Media and Political Engagement*. Washington, DC: Pew Internet & American Life Project, Pew Research Center. Accessed February 19, 2013. http://pewinternet.org/Reports/2012/Political-engagement.aspx.

Rapoza, Kenneth. 2011. "Fox News Viewers Uninformed, NPR Listeners Not, Poll Suggests." *Forbes*, November 21. Accessed May 29, 2013. http://www.forbes.com/sites/kenrapoza/2011/11/21/fox-news-viewers-uninformed-npr-listeners-not-poll-suggests/.

Rapp, Laura, Deanna Button, Benjamin Fleury-Steiner, and Ruth Fleury-Steiner. 2010. "The Internet as a Tool for Black Feminist Activism: Lessons from an Online Anti-Rape Protest." *Feminist Criminology* 5:244–62.

Rasmussen Reports. 2013. *52% View WikiLeaks Suspect Bradley Manning as a Traitor*. Asbury Park, NJ: Rasmussen Reports. Accessed September 3, 2013. http://www.rasmussenreports.com/public_content/politics/general_politics/june_2013/52_view_wikileaks_suspect_bradley_manning_as_a_traitor.

Reisinger, Don. 2008. "Stop the Insanity: CNN's 'Hologram' was Horrendous." CNET, November 6. Accessed May 10, 2013. http://news.cnet.com/stop-the-insanity-cnns-hologram-was-horrendous/.

Rheingold, Howard. 2002. *Smart Mobs: The Next Social Revolution*. Cambridge, MA: Basic Books.

Rice, Doyle. 2010. "Report: 97 Percent of Scientists Say Man-Made Climate Change Is Real." *USA Today*, June 22. Accessed April 14, 2013. http://content.usatoday.com/communities/sciencefair/post/2010/06/scientists-overwhelmingly-believe-in-man-made-climate-change/1#.UYhLroI1fw5.

Roach, John. 2013. "Global Warming Study Suggests Human Causes Dating Back to 1800s." *NBC News*, April 22. Accessed May 6, 2013. http://science.nbcnews.com/_news/2013/04/22/17864735-global-warming-study-suggests-human-causes-dating-back-to-1800s.

Roberts, Julian V. 1984. "Public Opinion and Capital Punishment: The Effects of Attitudes upon Memory." *Canadian Journal of Criminology* 26:283-91.

Rochon, Thomas R. 1998. *Culture Moves: Ideas, Activism, and Changing Values*. Princeton, NJ: Princeton University Press.

Rodham, Karen, Jeff Gavin, and Meriel Miles. 2007. "I Hear, I Listen and I Care: A Qualitative Investigation into the Function of a Self-Harm Message Board." *Suicide and Life-Threatening Behavior* 37:422–30.

Root, Wayne Allyn. 2012. "Real Lesson of the Chicago Teachers Strike—Fire Them All and Start Over!" Fox News, September 20. Accessed May 18, 2013. http://www.foxnews.com/opinion/2012/09/20/real-lesson-chicago-teachers-strike-fire-them-all-and-start-over/.

Rubin, Alissa J. 2007. "2 Iraqi Journalists Killed as U.S. Forces Clash with Militias." *The New York Times*, July 13. Accessed March 1, 2013. http://www.nytimes.com/2007/07/13/world/middleeast/13iraq.html.

Saad, Lydia. 2011. *More Americans Back Unions Than Governors in State Disputes*. Washington, DC: Gallup. Accessed May 20, 2011. http://www.gallup.com/poll/146921/Americans-Back-Unions-Governors-State-Disputes.aspx.

———. 2013. *More Americans Still Prioritize Economy over Environment*. Washington, DC: Gallup. April 3, 2013. Accessed April 16, 2013. http://www.gallup.com/poll/161594/americans-prioritize-economy-environment.aspx.

Sacco, Vincent F. 2005. *When Crime Waves*. Thousand Oaks, CA: Sage Publications.

Safire, William. 2004a. "Those Discredited Memos." *The New York Times*, September 13.

———. 2004b. "First, Find the Forger." *The New York Times*, September 22.

Savage, Charlie. 2013. "U.S. Weighs Wide Overhaul of Wiretap Laws." *The New York Times*, May 7.

Schneider, Joseph W. 1984. "Morality, Social Problems, and Everyday Life." In *Studies in the Sociology of Social Problems*, edited by Joseph W. Schneider and John I. Kitsuse, 180–206. Norwood, NJ: Ablex.

Schultz, Tanjev. 2000. "Mass Media and the Concept of Interactivity: An Exploratory Study of Online Forums and Reader Email." *Media, Culture, and Society* 22:205–21.

Seelye, Katharine Q. and Ralph Blumenthal. 2004. "Documents Suggest Guard Gave Bush Special Treatment." *The New York Times*, September 9.

Sengupta, Somini. 2013. "Concerns Arise on U.S. Effort to Allow Internet 'Wiretaps.'" *The New York Times*, May 16.

Shackle, Samira. 2012. "The Shooting of Malala Yousafzal Has Shocked an Unshockable Pakistan." *New Statesman*, October 10. Accessed November 10, 2012. http://www.newstatesman.com/blogs/world-affairs/2012/10/shooting-malala-yousafzai-has-shocked-unshockable-pakistan.

Shane, Scott and Andrew W. Lehren. 2010. "Leaked Cables Offer Raw Look at U.S. Diplomacy." *The New York Times*, November 29.

Shapira, Ian and Joby Warrick. 2010. "'WikiLeaks' Advocates are Wreaking 'Hacktivism.'" *The Washington Post*, December 12. Accessed February 25, 2013. http://www.washingtonpost.com/wp-dyn/content/article/2010/12/11/AR2010121102897.html.

Shawcross, Paul. 2013. "This Isn't the Petition Response You're Looking For." Last modified January 11. Accessed May 18, 2013. https://petitions.whitehouse.gov/response/isnt-petition-response-youre-looking.

Shelton, Sandi K. 2013. "Gun Control Activists Organize March for Change Thursday in Hartford." *New Haven Register*, February 12. Accessed March 17, 2013. http://www.nhregister.com/articles/2013/02/12/news/doc511aed0e8ea04521242452.txt.

Shirky, Clay. 2008. *Here Comes Everybody: The Power of Organizing Without Organizations.*" New York: Penguin Press.

Shoemaker, Pamela J. and Stephen D. Reese. 1996. *Mediating the Message: Theories of Influences on Mass Media Content*. White Plains, NY: Longman.

Shudson, Michael. 1996. "The Sociology of News Production Revisited." In *Mass Media and Society*, edited by James Curran and Michael Gurevitch, 141–59. London: Arnold.

Siddique, Haroon and Matthew Weaver. 2010. "US Embassy Cables Culprit Should Be Executed, Says Mike Huckabee." *The Guardian*, December 1. Accessed February 24, 2013. http://www.guardian.co.uk/world/2010/dec/01/us-embassy-cables-executed-mike-huckabee.

Sifry, Michael L. 2011. *WikiLeaks and the Age of Transparency*. New York: OR Books.

Silverman, Craig. 2010. "How WikiLeaks Outsourced the Burden of Verification." *Columbia Journalism Review*, July 30. Accessed March 2, 2013. http://cjr.org/campaign_desk/how_wikileaks_outsourced_the_b.php.

Simon, Johathan. 2007. *Governing Through Crime: How the War on Crime Transformed American Democracy and Created a Culture of Fear*. Oxford University Press.

Smith, Catharine. 2011. "Richard Engel Tweets Photo of Egyptian Protesters with 'Thank You Facebook' Sign." *The Huffington Post*, February 4. Accessed October 16, 2012. http://www.huffingtonpost.com/2011/02/04/egypt-protesters-thank-you-face-book_n_818745.html.

Smith, Tovia. 2013. "Political Attacks Ramp Up in U.S. Senate Race in Mass." WBUR, May 24. Accessed May 26, 2013. http://www.wbur.org/npr/186410381/political-attacks-ramp-up-in-mass-u-s-senate-race.

Snow, Robert P. 1983. *Creating Media Culture*. Beverly Hills: Sage.

Soulliere, Danielle M. 2003. "Prime-Time Murder: Presentations of Murder on Popular Television Justice Programs." *Journal of Criminal Justice and Popular Culture* 10:12–38.

Spector, Malcolm and John I. Kitsuse. 1977. "Social Problems: A Re-formulation." *Social Problems* 21:145–59.

Steinberg, Neil. 2013. "Mass Shootings Not a Big Problem." *Chicago Sun-Times*, April 4. Accessed April 7, 2013. http://www.suntimes.com/news/steinberg/19270756-452/mass-shootings-not-a-big-problem.html.

Stroud, Natalie J. 2010. "Polarization and Partisan Selective Exposure." *Journal of Communication* 60:556-76.

Surratt, Carla G. 2001. *The Internet and Social Change*. Jefferson, NC: McFarland & Company.

Tarrow, Sidney. 1996. "States and Opportunities: The Political Structuring of Social Movements." In *Comparative Perspectives on Social Movements*, edited by Doug McAdam, John D. McCarthy, and Mayer N. Zald, 41–61. New York: Cambridge University Press.

Taylor, Chris. 2011 "Why Not Call It a Facebook Revolution?" CNN, February 24. Accessed February 28, 2011. www.cnn.com/2011/TECH/social.media/02/24/facebook.revolution/index.html.

Tea Party Patriots. 2013. "Mainstream Media, Your Ideological Plagiarism Is Showing." Tea Party Patriots, September 6. Accessed September 8, 2013. http://www.teapartypatriots.org/2013/09/mainstream-media-your-ideological-plagiarism-is-showing/.

Tewksbury, David. 2003. "What Do Americans Really Want to Know? Tracking the Behavior of News Readers on the Internet." *Journal of Communication* 53:694–710.

Thompson, Hunter S. 1980. *Gonzo Papers, Vol. 1: The Great Shark Hunt: Strange Tales from a Strange Time*. New York: Summit Books.

Thompson, Nicholas. 2011. "Is Twitter Helping in Egypt?" *The New Yorker*, January 27. Accessed January 31, 2011. http://www.newyorker.com/online/blogs/newsdesk/2011/01/is-twitter-helping-in-egypt.html.

Trippi, Joe. 2004. *The Revolution Will Not Be Televised: Democracy, the Internet, and the Overthrow of Everything*. New York: HarperCollins.

Tuchman, Gaye. 1973. "Making News by Doing Work: Routinizing the Unexpected." *American Journal of Sociology* 79:110–31.

Ungar, Sheldon. 1992. "The Rise and (Relative) Decline of Global Warming as a Social Problem." *The Sociological Quarterly* 33:483–501.

United Press International. 2012. "NRA Shot and Missed in 2012 Election." *United Press International*, November 9. Accessed March 29, 2013. http://www.upi.com/Top_News/US/2012/11/09/NRA-shot-and-missed-in-2012-election/UPI-59931352473354/.

U.S. Senate. 2013. *Testimony of Wayne LaPierre Executive Vice President, National Rifle Association of America Before the U.S. Senate Committee on the Judiciary Hearing on "What Should America Do About Gun Violence?"* Washington, DC: Senate Judiciary Committee 113th Cong., 1st sess, U.S. Senate. Accessed April 4, 2013. http://www.judiciary.senate.gov/pdf/1-30-13LaPierreTestimony.pdf.

Useem, Bert and Mayer N. Zald. 1982. "Pressure Group to Social Movement: Organizational Dilemmas of the Effort to Promote Nuclear Power." *Social Problems* 30:144–56.

Van Aelst, Peter and Stefaan Walgrave. 2002. "New Media, New Movements? The Role of the Internet in Shaping the 'Anti-Globalization' Movement." *Information, Communication & Society* 5:465–93.

van Dijk, Teun A. 1996. "Power and the News Media." In *Political Communication and Action*, edited by David L. Paletz, 9–36. Cresskill, NJ: Hampton Press.

Vanobberghen, Wim. 2010. "'The Marvel of Our Time': Visions Surrounding the Introduction of Radio Broadcasting in Belgium in the Radio Magazine Radio (1923–28)." *Media History* 16:199–213.

Vargas, Jose A. 2009. "The Goracle: Al Gore, the Internet and the Future of American Politics." *The Huffington Post*, December 14. Accessed February 28, 2011. http://www.huffingtonpost.com/jose-antonio-vargas/the-goracle----al-gore-th_b_390892.html.

Vegh, Sandor. 2003. "Classifying Forms of Online Activism: The Case of Cyberprotests Against the World Bank." In *Cyberactivism: Online Activism in Theory and Practice*, edited by Martha McCaughey and Michael D. Ayers, 71–95. New York: Routledge.

Vollum, Scott and Jacqueline Buffington-Vollum. 2010. "An Examination of Social-Psychological Factors and Support for the Death Penalty: Attribution, Moral Disengagement, and the Value-Expressive Function of Attitudes." *American Journal of Criminal Justice* 35:15–36.

Walker, Peter. 2011. "Amnesty International Hails WikiLeaks and Guardian as Arab Spring 'Catalysts.'" *The Guardian*, May 12. Accessed February 12, 2013. http://www.guardian.co.uk/world/2011/may/13/amnesty-international-wikileaks-arab-spring.

Walsh, Michael. 2012. "Teacher Fired After Suggestive Photos of Unsuspecting Female Students Spotted on Reddit's Lurid Creepshots Forum, Investigation Underway." *New York Daily News*, September 28. Accessed February 22, 2013. http://www.nydailynews.com/news/national/teacher-fired-suggestive-photos-unsuspecting-female-students-spotted-reddit-lurid-creepshot-forum-investigation-underway-article-1.1170726.

The Washington Post. 2013. "How the NRA Exerts Influence over Congress." *The Washington Post*, January 15. Accessed March 29, 2013. http://www.washingtonpost.com/wp-srv/special/politics/nra-congress/.

Wathen, C. Nadine and Jacquelyn Burkell. 2002. "Believe It or Not: Factors Influencing Credibility on the Web." *Journal of the American Society for Information Science and Technology* 53:134–44.

Wau-Holland-Stiftung. 2012. *Project 04: Enduring Freedom of Information' Intermediate Transparency Report 2012 (January–June)*. Hamburg, Germany: Wau-Holland-Stiftung. Accessed February 21, 2013. http://wauland.de/files/2012-1_Transparenzbericht-Projekt04_en.pdf.

Weber, Joseph, 2012. "Solyndra, the Sequel? Bankrupt Solar Firm, DOE Facing Scrutiny over Panel Problems." Fox News, October 11. Accessed April 24, 2013. http://www.foxnews.com/politics/2012/10/11/another-bankrupt-solar-firm-facing-scrutiny-from-lawmakers-investigators/.

Webster, James G. 2005. "Beneath the Veneer of Fragmentation: Television Audience Polarization in a Multichannel World." *Journal of Communication* 55:366–82.

Welch, Chris. 2008. "Beam Me Up, Wolf! CNN Debuts Election-Night 'Hologram'." CNN, November 6. Accessed May 10, 2013. http://www.cnn.com/2008/TECH/11/06/hologram.yellin/.

Wellman, Barry, Anabel Quan Haase, James Witte, and Keith Hampton. 2001. "Does the Internet Increase, Decrease, or Supplement Social Capital? Social Networks, Participation, and Community Commitment." *American Behavioral Scientist* 45:436–55.

Wemple, Erik. 2013. "CNN's Double Breakdown: So Much for 'Abundance of Caution.'" *The Washington Post*, April 17. Accessed April 18, 2013. http://www.washingtonpost.com/blogs/erik-wemple/wp/2013/04/17/boston-bombing-suspect-cnn-double-breakdown-so-much-for-abundance-of-caution/.

Whalen, Jeanne and David Crawford. 2010. "How WikiLeaks Keeps Its Funding Secret." *The Wall Street Journal*, August 23. Accessed February 21, 2013. http://online.wsj.com/article/SB10001424052748704554104575436231926853198.html.

Wilcox, Miranda. 2013. "Facebook 'Terrorist' Released After Anonymous Donor Posts $500,000 Bail." *Houston Press*, July 18. Accessed September 8, 2013. http://blogs.houstonpress.com/hairballs/2013/07/good_samaritan_posts_500000_bo.php.

Williams, Bruce A. and Michael X. Delli Carpini. 2000. "Unchained Reaction: The Collapse of Media Gatekeeping and the Clinton-Lewinsky Scandal." *Journalism* 1:61–85.

———. 2004. "Monica and Bill All the Time and Everywhere." *American Behavioral Scientist* 47:1208–30.

Wright, Rachel A. and Hilary S. Boudet. 2012. "To Act or Not to Act: Context, Capability, and Community Response to Environmental Risk." *American Journal of Sociology* 118:728–77.

Wu, Tim. 2003 "Network Neutrality, Broadband Discrimination." *Journal of Telecommunications and High Technology Law* 2:141–79.

Yousafzal, Malala. 2009. "Diary of a Pakistani Schoolgirl." *BBC*, January 15–19. Accessed November 10, 2012. http://news.bbc.co.uk/2/hi/south_asia/7834402.stm.

Zeisel, Hans and Alec Gallup. 1989. "Death Penalty Sentiment in the United States." *Journal of Quantitative Criminology* 5:285–96.

Index

About the Author

R.J. Maratea is assistant professor of criminal justice at New Mexico State University. His research interests include mass communication, social problems, deviance, social control, and capital punishment. He is the author of several articles and book chapters on these topics, and his publications have appeared in *Social Problems*, *Symbolic Interaction*, and *Deviant Behavior*.

CPSIA information can be obtained at www.ICGtesting.com
Printed in the USA
BVOW08*1000121213

338842BV00001B/2/P